Affinity Publisher
for
Non-Fiction

AFFINITY PUBLISHER FOR
SELF-PUBLISHING - BOOK 4

M.L. HUMPHREY

SELECT TITLES BY M.L. HUMPHREY

CONTENTS

INTRODUCTION

Okay, first things first, if you haven't read *Affinity Publisher for Fiction Layouts*, you need to go read that first. Either that or you need to already be familiar with the basics of master pages, text styles, and how to flow text from one page to the next, as well as how to set up your workspace for working with print layouts.

This book assumes that you have a basic completed book that you're ready to add the bells and whistles to.

Second, the title of this book is a bit of a misnomer, because some of what we're going to cover here can also apply to fiction. For example, I have used a table of contents in my fantasy novels and if someone names their chapters they may well want to use those chapter names in their headers. But the rest is for non-fiction and it was a simpler title to use so there you have it.

So what are we going to cover in this book?

- How to create and format a table of contents

- How to use section or chapter names for the header instead of the book title

- How to have multiple columns of text on a page

- How to insert an index

- How to merge multiple book files into one

- How to insert images into the body of your text

It doesn't seem like a long list, but there's actually a lot of ground we're going to cover. And some of this stuff is the most finicky to work with. I have crashed the program more than once when trying to insert an index.

And I'm just going to warn you up front that these are also areas where I am personally the shakiest so I may not have the best answer on how to do these things. Of course, at this point I have formatted something like fifty non-fiction titles using Affinity Publisher, so when I say I'm shaky that's a personal standard not a general population standard.

Just know that there may be better ways to do the things I'm going to show you but I never got annoyed enough or curious enough to figure them out.

As an example, it took me until the last book I published to realize that there was an easier way to mark my index entries.

So if you're an expert at the stuff I listed above, this book may annoy you more than anything. But if you're stumbling through trying to make it all work and putting together little bits and pieces here or there like I tend to do when learning a new software, then this book should help accelerate your learning.

Okay then. Let's get started.

TABLE OF CONTENTS

Our first topic is going to be inserting and formatting a table of contents.

I'm first going to show you how to insert a basic, one-level table of contents. We'll then work our way through multi-level and customized table of contents and end with how to have multiple table of contents in one document.

A ONE-LEVEL TABLE OF CONTENTS

Here is an example of a one-level table of contents. This is pulled from *Affinity Publisher for Ad Creatives*:

There is one single line for each chapter with no sub-sections showing in the table of contents.

Also, it's not something you can see here, but all of those chapter names were formatted using the same text style so there was no need to incorporate multiple text styles when generating the table of contents.

PRE-PREP

Before we can create a table of contents like this we need to do some prep work. Specifically, we need a master page formatted to be our table of contents page. The header you see there, "Contents", is not provided by Affinity, you need to provide that part of things yourself.

Here you can see the full table of contents page in my document:

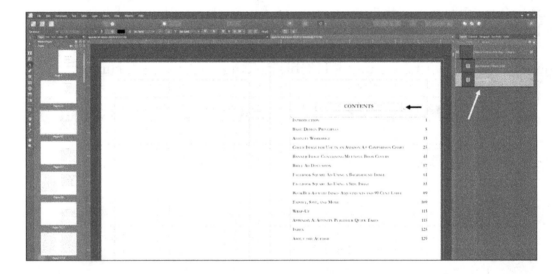

The master page for my table of contents has that text frame with "CONTENTS" in it and then another text frame below where I can drop in the actual table of contents.

Like so:

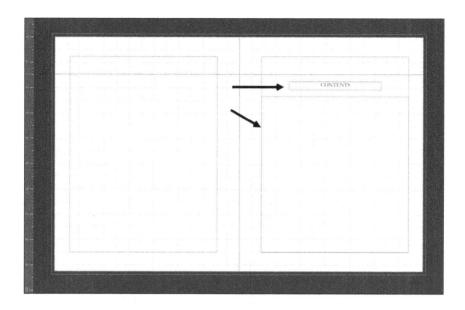

Which means your first step is to create the table of contents master page you want to use.

You can see that for mine I like to start the header a little lower on the page but not too far down, and that I leave a bit of space between that and where the actual table of contents text starts. Also, as mentioned, I use "CONTENTS" but you might want to use something else like "TABLE OF CONTENTS" or "CHAPTERS".

And you may want to have your copyright notice on the opposite page. I put my copyright notice opposite my Also By page so I leave the opposite page here blank.

Whatever you want, go format it now.

Once you have that set up, insert your table of contents master page in your document where you want your table of contents to be.

For me this is after my copyright and Also By page. I just glanced at a few of the books on my shelves and many of them put the table of contents after a dedications and acknowledgment page. Whatever works for you. I assume most would agree it should be before your main content starts and probably as close to that start point as you can get.

(Remember we're doing a singular table of contents right now for the whole book.)

That was prep step one.

Prep step two is to have a text style or styles that you've applied to the text you want to include in your table of contents. This style should not be applied to any other text in your document. Because Affinity won't be able to distinguish the difference between what you want to include or not include. So even if the formatting is identical between the text you want to include and other text in your document, you need to use separate styles for those two groups.

Since this is a one-level table of contents, that's generally going to be your chapter header text style.

In my case, it's showing as CSP-Chapter Title 1 because at some point I must've brought over text from an old KDP Word CreateSpace template.

I mention that there can be multiple text styles because sometimes that happens. Especially for novels I will use a different text style for my main chapters than I use for my back matter, like my About the Author section.

Affinity can work with multiple text styles, you just need to know going in that there are multiple styles involved and make sure that those styles are only applied to text you want to include.

But let's start simple with just one text style.

So at this point you should have a master page designed for your table of contents and you should have a specific text style assigned to your chapter headers. Now we're ready to create our table of contents.

INSERT A TABLE OF CONTENTS

Go to the page spread that's going to hold your table of contents and click into the location on the page where you want to insert it.

You now have two choices for how to do so.

Option one is to go to Text in the top set of menu options and then to Table of Contents in the dropdown menu and from there choose Insert Table of Contents. So Text->Table of Contents->Insert Table of Contents.

Option two is to go into the Table of Contents studio (which is one of the studios I have docked on the top left of my workspace if you're using my set-up from *Affinity Publisher for Fiction Layouts*) and click on the Insert option there which looks like three pages stacked with the middle one filled in:

The initial result you see may be "No Table of Contents Entries Found":

That is because you need to tell Affinity which style to use to identify the table of content entries. Its default is going to likely be Heading 1 and maybe Heading 2, so if those aren't the styles you're using for your chapter headers it won't pick them up.

You need to do this in the Table of Contents studio, but good news is that if you didn't already have it open, trying to insert a table of contents will have opened it for you. Here is the top portion of the studio:

You'll need to scroll down though to get to the section we want right now.

My docked version of the studio shows more of the available options, including the most important part right now, the Style Name section that includes check boxes for each style.

Note that in my screenshot none of the listed styles are currently selected. That's because Affinity does not yet know which text style is the one I want to use for my table of contents. In a file that's completely new you may see that Heading 1 and Heading 2 are checked.

Go into this section, find the text style you applied to your headers, and click the checkbox on the left to select that text style.

If other styles that you didn't use are also checked, like Heading 1 and Heading 2, you can uncheck those or ignore them if they didn't bring in any entries to your table of contents.

When you check or uncheck the Style Names in the Table of Contents studio, Affinity will automatically adjust your table of contents for you. Like so:

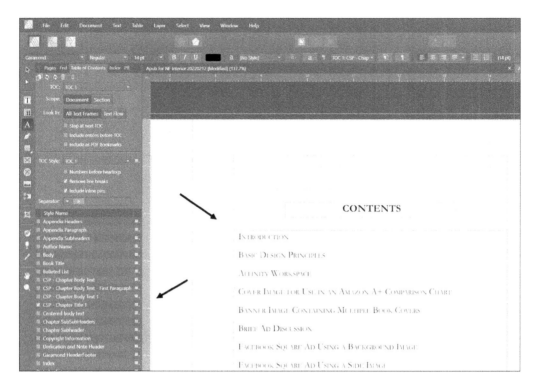

(Note that the formatting here is not what you will see. I'm using a document that had formatting already applied to the table of contents so that's what's showing for me. Below you'll see an example of the default formatting.)

INCLUDE MULTIPLE TEXT STYLES

If you want to incorporate text using more than one text style, simply check the boxes for all of the style names you want to use and those entries will be included in the table of contents.

In a file that's previously had a formatted table of contents using one of the text styles, the entries in the table of contents may not all look the same, but in a completely new file they should, like they do here:

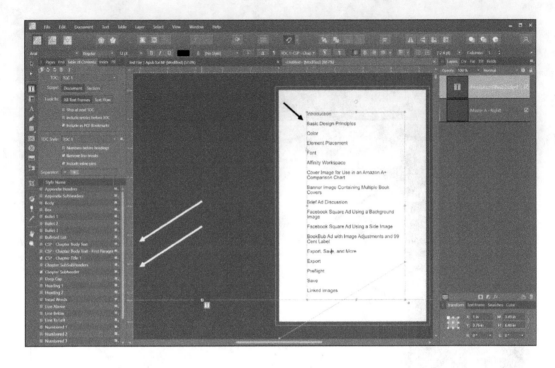

This is a brand new file that I pasted my text into to see what happens when there's no pre-existing formatting working behind the scenes.

I want you to note two things here.

First, that the formatting in the table of contents is identical for both text styles I've selected, CSP – Chapter Title 1 and Chapter Subheader.

And second, that the style assigned to both is TOC 1 which by default uses Arial, Regular, 12 pt.

This formatting differs from the one I was just showing you in my document. That is because I'm using a document where I've already adjusted my table of contents formatting to use Garamond and Small Caps.

Let's walk through how to make formatting changes like that in your document.

FORMATTING

PAGE NUMBERS

First off, I want page numbers for my entries.

To add page numbers, be sure you're clicked into the table of contents in your document so that the Table of Contents studio is active, and then go to the studio and find the style name you checked. Go to the end of the row with that style name listed where you can see four white lines with a dropdown arrow on the bottom right corner.

Click on that arrow and you should see a very small dropdown menu where you can click on the box next to "Include Page Number".

That should give you something like this where there are now page numbers at the end of each entry in the table of contents in your document:

Do this for each text style used in the table of contents. (Assuming you want page numbering to show for all of your entries.)

TEXT

We have page numbers now, but I don't like the default formatting Affinity uses.

The easiest way to change the formatting is to select some of the text in the table of contents in your document and change it there just like you would any other text.

So I'm going to highlight "Introduction" in my table of contents and then go to the Character studio and click the box for small caps and change the font to Garamond. The font selection and size are available up top, the all caps or small caps options are in the Typography section.

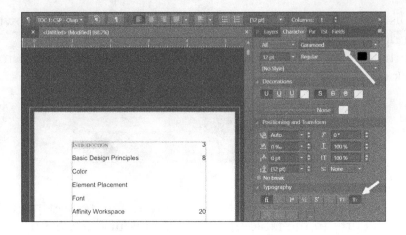

Small caps is the last option in the row. All caps is the one right before that.

I happen to like small caps. I would suggest using small caps or all caps in your table of contents, simply because they gloss over any issues around which words should be capitalized and which shouldn't in a title.

If you don't use one of those two formats, the capitalization of the text in your table of contents will match that of the entries the text is pulled from. Which means that if you ever see that you have a capitalization issue in your table of contents, you should ideally change it in the main body of the document, not the table of contents.

You can make any changes you want to the text in the table of contents once that text has been inserted, but the issue is that those changes will be overwritten if you ever update your table of contents again.

That's why it's a really bad idea to do extensive edits directly to the table of contents. It's very easy to forget you did so, see in preflight that Affinity thinks you should update your table of contents, click on the button to do so, and then lose all of your manual table of contents edits.

Much better to fix them in such a way that an automatic update doesn't change anything.

Speaking of…

UPDATE TOC TEXT STYLE

It was great that I could make those edits to the formatting of "Introduction", but I now want to apply those changes to all of my table of contents entries. And I also want to do so in such a way that I won't lose that formatting if I ever update the table.

To make that happen I need to update the text style used by Affinity for my table of contents entries.

While clicked onto that newly-formatted text entry, go to the dynamic menu up top, and click on the Update Paragraph Style option which is the little paragraph mark next to the current style name that has a swish mark:

You can see that the text style applied to this text right now was TOC 1:... which is a table of contents-specific text style. Updating that style to match the edits I just made will update all table of contents entries that are using that same style:

But note how in the screenshot above the second line updated to match the formatting I applied to Introduction, but the next three lines didn't.

That's because the content of those three lines was pulled from a different text style in my document and the table of contents treats them separately.

(Remember I had the Style Name boxes for both Chapter Title and Chapter Subheader checked in the Table of Contents studio.)

This is easy enough to fix. I can just format one of those entries the exact same way and then update that style as well.

Or if I wanted it to be slightly different, the fact that Affinity treats them as separate styles allows me to do that. So let's say I want a different font size for that one. I'm going to make it Garamond, 10 pt, and put it in all caps instead of small caps.

Here we go:

INDENT

But now I have an issue. It's not very easy to distinguish the subheader entries from the rest. The all caps and font size difference just don't make it stand out much.

What I really want is for those subheader entries to be indented, but when I try that indent level option in the Table of Contents studio, it doesn't do anything. What I can do, though, is select a line of that text in the table of contents, go to the Paragraph studio, and set a left indent of .2.

Update my text style and this is what I get:

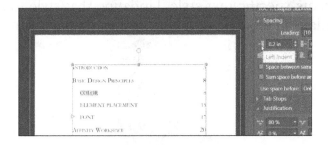

That's better. It sets those sub-entries apart nicely.

I showed you that because basically any formatting you can do on normal text you can also do on your table of contents entries. Just remember to update the style to keep those changes so they aren't lost if you update your table of contents later.

For me that would probably be good enough and I'd be done, but there are a few more formatting items I want to mention.

SPACE AND SEPARATORS BETWEEN TEXT AND PAGE NUMBERS

The Separator option in the Table of Contents studio is where you can tell Affinity how to separate your text from your page numbers.

Here, for example, I've removed the Tab separator and just used an Em Dash to separate the text from the numbers.

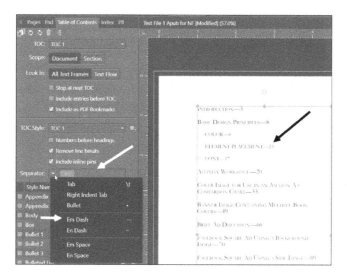

Not my preference, but an option. As is any combination of the elements in that list.

On this particular table of contents some of the page numbers ended up on the left-hand side because of the text taking up too much of the line.

To fix that you could manually adjust it by highlighting the page number and then choosing right-align to format it.

But that is a manual adjustment that will be overridden each time you refresh the table of contents unless you update the page number text style.

I poked around a bit for a solution on this one and think that I stumbled across something that works. It was to have an Em Space followed by a Tab in the Separator section. That seemed to work for the table of contents I have here, but no promises it will work for any other set-up:

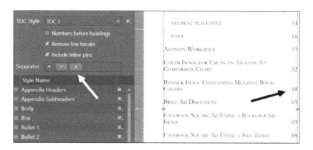

You can also click into that field next to Separator and manually type in something like a space or a period. Like here where I added a few periods in a row:

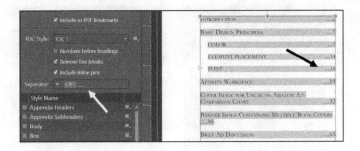

Again not my favorite. And I will note here that after I typed each period it kicked me out of the field, so I had to type a period, click back into the field, type the next one, etc. So not only not great looking, but not easy to do.

If you want to add a dotted line all the way across, though, there's an easier way to do it.

Click on the text for one of your table of contents entries, go to the Text Styles studio, right-click on the table of contents entry option for that style or for all entries (in this example, TOC 1: Entry), and choose Edit from the dropdown menu.

That is going to bring up the Edit Text Style dialogue box. On the left-hand side under Paragraph there is a listing for Tab Stops. Click on it.

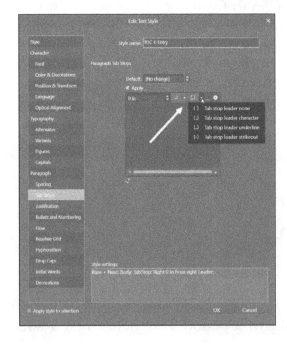

There should be a tab stop entry already showing under Paragraph Tab Stops. Click on the second dropdown arrow, the one next to the set of parens, and choose the option for tab stop leader character which has a period within the parens.

You will get a result that looks like this where there are periods between the end of the table of contents entry and the page number:

If there wasn't a tab stop entry already you can click on the + sign below the box to add one.

If you choose the TOC 1: Entry text style that will edit all of your table of content styles at once. If you just want the dotted line for one of your styles then make your edits to that particular text style instead.

That was how to add a dotted line. That dropdown also gives you the option to add a solid line at either underline height or strikeout height.

The Tab Stops section of the Edit Text Style dialogue box is also where you can adjust the amount your page numbers are indented from the right side of the text frame. You do this by increasing the value for the position setting from its default of zero.

You can also have multiple tab stops if you need them.

PAGE NUMBER FORMATTING

Page numbers do have their own text style. By default it will mirror the text style for the corresponding entry, but you can edit it directly if that's ever needed, like above with the right-alignment setting I mentioned to ensure your page numbers are always on the right-hand side.

Okay, so that was formatting.

UPDATE YOUR TABLE OF CONTENTS

It is very likely that after you initially insert your table of contents you will need to update it at some point. Maybe you add or delete some text, or change a chapter name to fix a typo, or add some back matter. Whatever the reason, you will very likely need to update your table of contents before you are through.

Your first option is to go to the Table of Contents studio and click on the update option at the top:

There are actually two update options to choose from. When you only have one table of contents in your document it doesn't really matter which one of them you use, they both do the same thing. (Once you have multiple table of contents the update one should apply to the currently listed table of contents, the other will update all table of contents in the document. We'll cover this in a bit.)

Your second option is to go to Text-> Table of Contents and choose to update the table of contents from there.

Your final option is in the Preflight studio. There will often be a message at the top that "One or more tables of contents entries need updating." Simply click on "Fix" to update the table of contents that way.

Whichever method you use, be sure to visually review your table of contents again afterward to make sure you didn't have any manual change to the table of contents that has now been erased.

Okay, so that was the basics of a single table of contents with one or more levels of entries. Now let's talk about multiple table of contents. This is trickier and we'll cover it again when we talk about merging multiple books into one.

MULTIPLE TABLE OF CONTENTS

I use multiple table of contents when I am publishing a collection of non-fiction titles. I generally don't need this for omnibus editions of my fiction titles, but again, if someone uses chapter titles and wants to list those out at the beginning of each novel then they might need multiple tables of contents to do so.

But for me, for example, my *Excel Essentials 2019* series has three books in it that I've published separately that are part of the published collection. That collection has one overarching table of contents where I list the name of each individual title and its starting page number as well as the back matter and then at the beginning of each individual title I have the book-specific table of contents.

So here's the overarching table of contents:

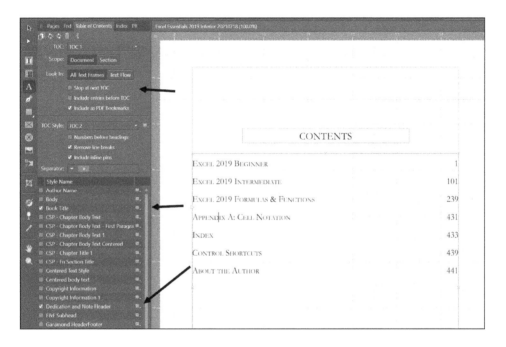

The key things to note here are that I used two text styles for this main table of contents. They don't look any different in the actual table of contents, but definitely are in the book itself since the book titles are pulled from a title page and the back matter entries are simple chapter headings.

Since I wanted my back matter, like the about the author section and my control shortcuts, to be in this first table of contents, I assigned a different text style from my chapter headers to those entries in the document.

So that's step one in a situation like this. Figure out what you want to include in that main table of contents and then make sure that all of the text that you want to include has a text style assigned to it that is not assigned to any other text in your document.

You can have multiple text styles that feed into the main table of contents, but make sure those text styles are not assigned to any other text in the document.

The second thing I want to note here is that for the main, overarching table of contents you want to NOT check that "Stop at next TOC" box. Because the entries in this table of contents are likely going to be drawing from the entire book.

And you can see here that that's true. My first table of contents entry is coming from page 1 but my last one is coming from page 441 and there are three books' worth of content in between the two.

Now let's look at the table of contents for the first book in this collection, *Excel 2019 Beginner.*

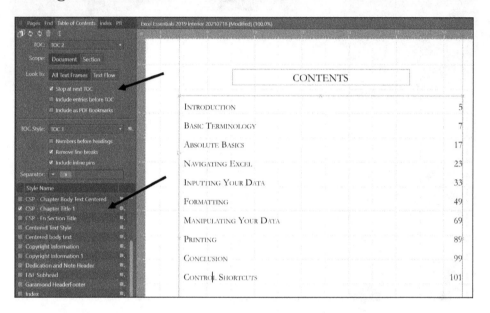

The text style used for this table of contents is different from the text styles used for the main table of contents. This text style can be used throughout the main body of the document. It's used for all of my chapters in all three books.

It works that way because of the second setting I want you to notice here. For the secondary tables of contents, I do check the "Stop at next TOC" box. That allows Affinity to pull all of my chapter headers from this title, but to stop pulling entries at the table of contents for the next title in the collection.

Here is that second book-specific table of contents:

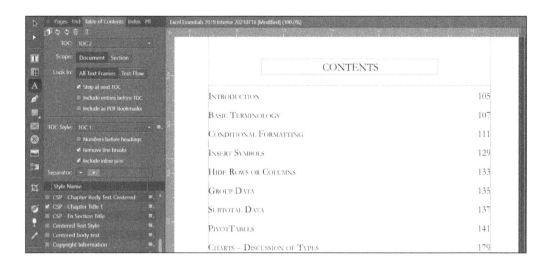

Note how it begins on page 105? And the prior table of contents stopped on page 101?

That's because we told Affinity to stop at the next table of contents. The style name used for this table of contents is the same as the style name used for the first title table of contents.

Note that the box for "include entries before TOC" is also not checked. That's the case by default and you should never have to even think about it, but I mention here just in case. You want the table of contents contained to entries for this title only.

So that's it. The key to having multiple table of contents is (1) using different text styles for the overarching table of contents versus the other table of contents, (2) letting the overarching table of contents pull entries from the entire book, and (3) limiting the additional table of contents to only their section by clicking on "Stop at next TOC" and not including entries from before each TOC.

Sometimes this will require making adjustments. Usually I have to change the text style for my back matter to a new text style, for example. But it's usually not too much work. You'll see this in action when we reach the chapter on merging existing books into one.

Also, you can have different formatting for each Style Name in each table of contents in your document. These happen to be formatted the same way, but Affinity assigns a different text style for each Style Name in each table of contents, so each one is fully customizable by itself.

MULTI-PAGE TABLE OF CONTENTS

One final issue to mention. Sometimes you'll have a table of contents that flows across multiple pages so you'll want to create a master page or master pages for that scenario.

I have two additional master pages, one for two pages of table of contents entries and one for a single page of table of contents entries and a chapter start page.

There should be text flow between your table of contents pages but not between the table of contents and your first chapter. I also include a "CONTENTS (CONT.)" header as well as page numbering on all subsequent table of contents pages.

Once you have those master pages, simply insert the one(s) you need after the initial table of contents master page and then flow your text from that first page to the others.

Here for example is the end of a five-page table of contents:

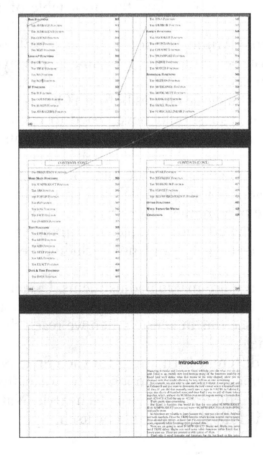

You can see the blue lines that connect the table of contents pages, but note how the final page of the table of contents does not flow forward from there. I do not connect my table of contents to the main body of my book.

You can also see that I let the subsequent pages in my table of contents take up the whole page when I set up my master pages.

Also note that for a table of contents that's at the beginning of the book, page numbering should be in lower-case Roman numerals (ii, iii, iv, etc.). But for a table of contents later in a book, like this one, the page numbering just continues from the prior page. So here the pages are 242, 243, etc.

Basically, you have one set of numbers for your intro material and another for the rest of the book. We'll cover this more in the merging existing titles chapter.

* * *

For now that should be the end of our discussion of table of contents. Let's move on to an easier subject, using chapter names for your headers instead of your book title.

USE CHAPTER NAMES FOR HEADERS

I now want to talk about how to have different headers for each of your chapters or sections rather than just using the book title throughout the whole book.

(And I'm going to say headers throughout this section, but if for some reason you put the book title or chapter names in your footers or on the side of the page instead, it works the same way there. Basically anywhere you'd have Affinity auto-populate your book title you can instead have it auto-populate using your section names.)

Like here where you can see that my chapter name is Introduction and the odd-numbered pages in that section also have Introduction for the header. (As opposed to the book name which is how we set up the fiction book we did in *Affinity Publisher for Fiction Layouts*.)

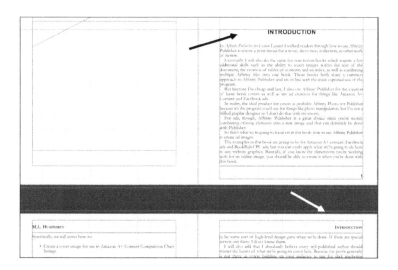

The first step is to modify any of your impacted master pages.

For me that's just my Text and Text master page. That's the only master page I have for non-fiction that has book title or section title text in the header since I start all of my chapters on the right-hand side of the page for non-fiction.

If you were doing this for fiction chapter names, which you could, and you were letting your chapter starts fall where they may, then you'd probably have a chapter start and text master page that also needed edited.

And depending on how you've formatted your back matter master pages, one of those may also require an edit. (You'll catch it in the PDF review if you miss it now, but this is why you need to scan through the entire final file when you're done because one page can look fine and then another that uses a different master page will not.)

Okay. Chances are, if you followed *Affinity Publisher for Fiction Layouts*, you have a text and text master page that looks something like this where the actual title of your book shows in the right-hand header of the master page:

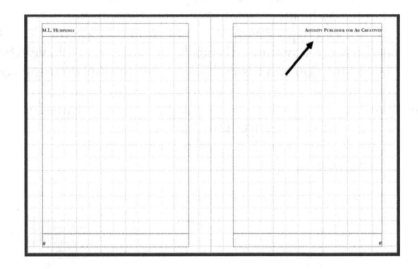

That's actually using a field to populate the text, but because the title is the same throughout the document Affinity just shows the title itself rather than the field marker for book title in the master page. (I would personally prefer they didn't do it that way, but it is what it is.)

To use the chapter names instead, what we actually need to do is tell Affinity to use section names. I refer to this as the chapter names because that's how I break up my sections, but technically sections do not have to be tied to chapters. So you could have a section that encompasses ten chapters and use that name in your headers or you could split a chapter into three sections and use those names instead.

But for the sake of simplicity, I'm going to talk about chapters.

First step, go to the Master Pages section of the Pages studio and double-click on the master page you want to edit to open it in your workspace.

Next, click on the Artistic Text Tool (the capital A on the left-hand side) and then click into the text frame where you have your book title and highlight and delete it.

If you didn't have text to delete, just click into that text frame. Now go to the menu up top, and under Text->Insert->Fields, choose Section Name.

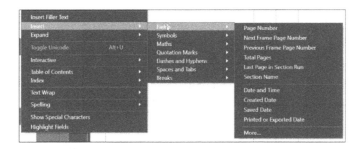

Your master page should look like this now with the <Section Name> in place of your book title. The <> marks indicate that this is a field that will be populated with a value in the actual document:

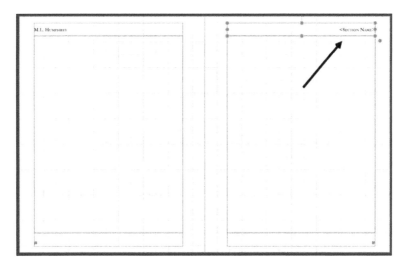

Do this for every master page where you need to change out the book title for the section name or want to add a section name.

That was step one. Affinity won't bring in section names to your final document unless you've specified a location for it to use. But chances are, you really don't have any section names for it to bring in at this point, because you didn't need sections for each chapter before this.

If you were just using the book title then the only sections you probably used were for your front matter where the page numbering needed to be different. For example, here are the sections I have in my large print version for my first cozy mystery:

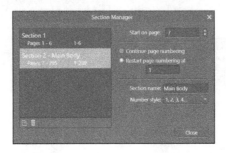

There are only two of them and only one has an assigned name.

Which means for a book that uses chapter/section names instead of book title in the header, we've got some work to do.

Here, for example, is the Section Manager for *Affinity Publisher for Fiction Layouts*:

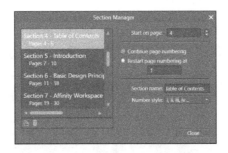

It has seventeen sections, because in order to have my headers show Introduction, Basic Design Principles, Affinity Workspace, etc. I had to go into Affinity and create sections for each of my chapters.

One thing to keep in mind when working with sections is that every single page in your document will be part of a section. If a document is 100 pages long and you start a section on page 10 and don't add any other sections then pages 1-9 will be one section and pages 10 through 100 will be another.

This means if I only want pages 10 to 20 to be part of a section, then I need to go to page 21 and assign a new section there even if I'm not going to see that section name anywhere in my final document.

For the most part that's not going to be an issue for you. You'll naturally have all of those breaks because we're going to assign a section for each chapter start. But at the very end of the book you may want to watch out for this because you could have "Conclusion" carry over into your back matter. Also, if you have any section divider pages throughout the document you may want those to have their own section.

A lot of it will come down to which master pages you're using and whether they're set to show a book title or section name. You can have messed up sections as long as the master pages aren't set to show that fact in the final product.

Still. Keep it in mind when assigning sections and when troubleshooting errant header or page numbering that you didn't want. There's nothing wrong with having more sections than you need to ensure that you keep things clean.

Okay. Let's go through now and do step two which is assigning new sections to each of our chapters and providing our section names.

Go to your first chapter start in the Pages section of the Pages studio, right-click on that singular page (not the two-page spread), and choose Start New Section from the dropdown menu.

This will bring up the Section Manager dialogue box:

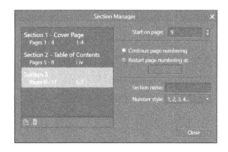

Our chapter is Section 3, because we already had sections for the cover page and the table of contents.

We've already told Affinity where to start this section, on the first page of the chapter. But now we need to tell Affinity the Section Name we want to use in the header. Click on the space next to Section Name and it will turn into a white input field.

You want to put in that field the actual text you'd like to see in the header.

Usually I can just copy and paste the chapter name into that field and I'm fine. But watch out for situations where you have a chapter name that is too long for the header text frame. In that case you'll want to choose a header that's a little more reasonable.

Like here where you can see from the table of contents that my actual chapter name is "Cover Image for Use in an Amazon A+ Comparison Chart" but I changed the header to just "Amazon A+ Comparison Chart":

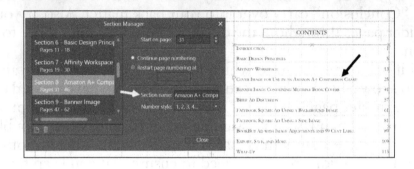

I should note here that when I run into this issue it is often a sign to me that I should actually modify the chapter name to something simpler.

In early drafts I'm a little too fond of titling chapters with things like "Learn to Create a ..." or "Insert a..." when I could just simply list the chapter name as whatever they are going to insert or learn to create.

But I still do end up with overly-lengthy chapter names even when I make those changes, so I still have to keep an eye on the actual final product to make sure my text fully shows up in my header.

(And I will note this is one of the reasons I moved away from using Vellum for print because I once bought a non-fiction book that had been created in Vellum and used long chapter names and Vellum had just cut off the end of the chapter name in the header and put ... at the end. It was not a good look. And not something I could figure out how to control in that program.)

Back to our chapter sections. You need a new section for every time you want to change what the header text will display. And you need to put in that Section Name field whatever text it is you want displayed for that section.

For the first chapter of your book, also make sure you restart your page numbering at 1 and change back to Arabic numerals (1, 2, 3...) from Roman in the Number Style dropdown if that isn't the case already.

For every chapter or section after that point the numbering should continue the page numbering and use Arabic numerals. I don't think you'll have to change this, I think it will be automatic, but check to be sure as you're creating your sections.

(And for section dividers and things like that where you don't want a page number showing on the page, that's handled in your master page layout not here. Simply don't include a place for page number on the master page that you use for those.)

You shouldn't have to specify the ending page for your sections, because those will be set by the starting page for the next section. So as long as you add new sections throughout, that should be taken care of automatically.

As you add each section, the title you provided for that section should appear wherever you have your section name field on your master page. This does mean that for some shorter chapters you'll never actually see the section name in your document. Still create that section, though. Because if you add a little bit of text to a chapter and it pushes it to three pages long, suddenly you're going to need to have assigned that section name.

If you later notice an issue with one of your section titles or the page numbering used in a section, you can simply right-click on any page in the Pages section of the Pages studio and choose Edit Section to re-open the Section Manager. The Section Manager covers the entire document, so once it's open you can edit any section you want.

Simply click on the section you need to edit and change whatever you need to change.

The two changes we haven't discussed yet are deleting a section, which you can do by clicking on that section name and then using the trash can below the listing of sections. Here:

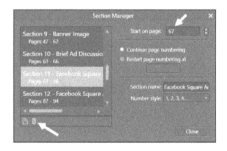

And changing the "start on page" value for the section which you can do at the top of the dialogue box. See the arrow above. That will shift the end of the prior section as well. Remember, every page has to be assigned to a section. Also, each page can only be assigned to one section.

You can also add a new section directly in the Section Manager dialogue box, but I prefer to do so from within the Pages studio. The Section Manager dialogue box uses the page number for each page based upon the entire document length. So Chapter 5 may be on page 47 according to the Section Manager but I see it in my formatted document as page 36.

Rather than try to do that mental gymnastics, I'd rather just to go to the page for Chapter 5, right-click, and insert the section that way.

But if you're more confident about those things than me, you can use the little page icon next to the trash can below the listing of the current sections in the Section Manager to insert your new section. And then you'd need to provide the start on page as well as any edits to the number style, whether the page numbering continues or not, and the section name.

Okay, so that's it.

To use section/chapter names in your headers you first modify your master pages and then assign sections and section names throughout your document.

MULTIPLE COLUMNS ON A PAGE

Those first two items were ones that could apply to fiction books as well as non-fiction. There's one more topic like that, merging multiple books into one title, so if you're dealing with fiction you may want to skip ahead to that chapter.

Right now we're going to turn our attention to a few tricks that apply more to non-fiction books, specifically having more than one column on the page and indexes.

We'll cover multiple columns first.

I use this one for my Index section in each book because most of my index entries are pretty short and I don't need to take up a full line for each of them. I'd end up with a ten-page index that had a lot of white space on the page.

Here's an example of an index page from one of my books:

INDEX	
A	Export 110
Affinity Help 107–108	PDF 64, 103–105, 110
Author Name 109	I
Field Edit 109	Image 110
Insert 109	Adjustments 97–101, 110
B	Border 95
Book Title 109	Center 110
Field Edit 109	DPI 83, 86, 91, 110
Insert 109	Float 93–94, 110

This is the index page with text frames showing. And it is the top of the first page of the index.

You can see that the entries start in the left-hand column and go downward, there's then a space between that column and the second column, and then the entries continue in that second column on the right-hand side.

In this case, both of the columns are the same width.

I set this up on the master page for my index, so it's already built in when I use it.

It's very easy to do. Go to the master page where you want multiple columns, and if you don't already have one there, insert a text frame onto your page. If you already have a text frame, make sure it's selected.

Next, find the Columns option at the far right side of the dynamic menu up top and change the value from 1 to 2 or whichever number of columns you want to use:

Affinity will take that text frame and create that number of columns for you in that space using the default settings, which are what you saw in my screenshot above. You can customize those settings, however.

Next to the Columns option is an option for specifying the width of the gap between your columns.

In my screenshot above that setting is currently hidden and I need to either click on the double-arrow at the very end of the dynamic menu to see more options or widen my Affinity window to make it visible.

Here I went ahead and widened the window but you can still see that there are more options behind that double-arrow at the end:

The gutter width setting is right next to the number of columns setting. You can change that setting to zero if you want no gap between the two columns (not something I'd recommend unless you have other settings on your text to maintain some distance) or you can increase the gap if you don't think it's big enough as is.

If you resize your text frame by clicking and dragging from the right-hand side, that will also resize all of your columns. The gutter will not change when you do this, though.

If you want to get really detailed or have different-sized columns, you can open the Text Frame studio and go to the Columns section there:

As an example, I'm going to create a layout with two equally-sized columns and one smaller third column.

As I change the first column that automatically changes the other columns to keep the same total width as I started with because the "Preserve Width" box is checked. If I didn't want that, I could uncheck that box and then the width of the text frame would just be the total of my column widths and gutters.

Below is an example of two larger columns and one smaller.

It didn't let me have uneven gutters so those had to stay the same but you can see that my first and second columns are 2.327 inches and then my last one is .946 inches with a .2 inch gutter between the columns:

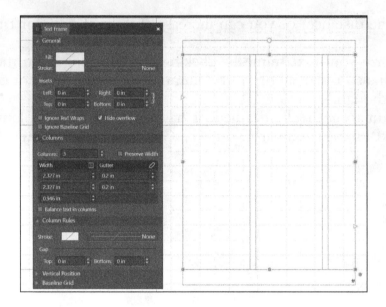

It's also possible to have a visible line dividing your columns. You can create one by using the Stroke setting in the Column Rules section of the Text Frame studio.

Click on the line with the red mark through it next to the Stroke color box and then change the Width value to a non-zero value.

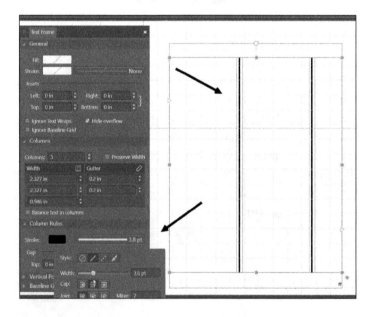

Here I've changed it to 3.8 pt and you can see that there are now dark black lines in the gutters between my columns. I used the Width slider until I could visibly see lines between the columns but you could as easily enter a specific value.

In that same Stroke dialogue box, if you go to Start and End you can change the settings there so that the line has a shape at the end.

And if you don't want the line to extend from top to bottom but to just fill part of the space, you can set the Top and Bottom values under Gap in the Column Rules section to create a shorter line.

Here I've changed the lines to have an arrow at each end and to have a 1.25 inch gap at the top and bottom:

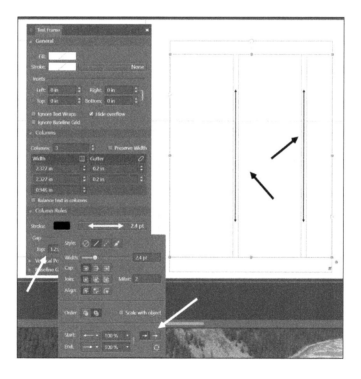

There's a lot you can play with in this section, but honestly I just normally keep it simple. No lines, no arrows, no gaps. Just two columns equally spaced.

There is one final setting that may come in handy, though, and that's the checkbox to "Balance Text in Columns" which is in the Columns section of the Text Frame studio just below the column measurements we covered above.

This comes into play when you don't have enough text to fill the entire page. You can check this box and Affinity will evenly spread what text there is across however many columns you have.

Here's an example with two columns.

This first example is balanced. You can see that the text in both columns ends at about the same point on the page:

weights for that font. Or select text and go to Character studio font weight dropdown at top.

TEXT FRAME

ALIGN OR POSITION

Frame Text Tool or Move Tool. Left-click on text frame and hold as you drag. Look for red and green alignment lines to center or align to other elements in workspace. (Turn on Snapping if there are no red or green lines.) Use Alignment dropdown in top menu to align to workspace, not the dynamic menu bar that applies to actual text.

INSERT

Frame Text Tool on left-hand side.

Click and drag in workspace.

RESIZE

Click on text frame layer. Left-click and drag on one of the blue circles around the perimeter of the text. Click and drag at an angle from the corner to keep scaling proportionate.

UNDO

Ctrl + Z. Or you can open the History studio and rewind using the slider or by clicking back onto a prior step.

This second example is not balanced and just lets the text fall where it may:

weights for that font. Or select text and go to Character studio font weight dropdown at top.

TEXT FRAME

ALIGN OR POSITION

Frame Text Tool or Move Tool. Left-click on text frame and hold as you drag. Look for red and green alignment lines to center or align to other elements in workspace. (Turn on Snapping if there are no red or green lines.) Use Alignment dropdown in top menu to align to workspace, not the dynamic menu bar that applies to actual text.

INSERT

Frame Text Tool on left-hand side. Click and drag in workspace.

RESIZE

Click on text frame layer. Left-click and drag on one of the blue circles around the perimeter of the text. Click and drag at an angle from the corner to keep scaling proportionate.

I should also note here that when I was trying to check and uncheck that balance box sometimes it didn't seem to take. So always be sure you've clicked on your text frame before you make the adjustment, because it seems a little finicky. (Or it could be me.)

Also, when I had the three columns set up I wasn't able to get Affinity to not flow text to that final column. So if what you actually want is a layout that has, for example, a third column for pull-out quotes or something like that, then columns are not the way to go.

In that instance what you'd want are two linked text frames for your main body text and then a third text frame that is standalone for any pullout text.

Okay, so that was columns. Now let's talk talk about how to create an index in your document.

INDEXES

Now on to indexes, which should probably be called indices instead, but I don't like indices as much as I like indexes. And this is my book so I get to do what I want. (And it turns out the dictionary thinks I'm okay doing it that way. They're both acceptable.)

Inserting an index into an Affinity document is where I have encountered the most crashes and had the most challenges. This could very much be a me issue not a them issue. But it's a fact that I used to crash my files on a regular basis when inserting an index.

Fortunately, Affinity's recovery settings are excellent and I rarely lost anything. Also, I finally figured out a workaround that seems to solve my personal issue, which was that I would accidentally insert an index into my document in the wrong location when I was actually trying to mark a new entry for the index, and when I would then try to undo that using Ctrl + Z it would crash the program instead.

I rarely lost anything other than that index I didn't want there anyway, but I had to train myself to never ever use Undo if I accidentally inserted an index where I didn't want it.

The more long-term solution to this issue was to flag one entry for my index, go to where I did want my index inserted, and insert the index immediately. That prevented me from accidentally inserting an index into the document instead of marking an entry later, because Affinity only allows one index and I already had one.

When I was done marking all my index entries I then just had to update that index so it reflected all of my entries. (Which sometimes required deleting the existing entries before it would work, but since it was one entry that wasn't too hard to do.)

I'll also note here that you may not even have to update your index at the end. On the last index I inserted into a document, it automatically updated for me as I tagged new entries.

Hopefully crashing Affinity when using an index will not be an issue for you, but I wanted to cover it up front so you understand why I'm approaching this in what may seem like a weird way.

This is also definitely one of the areas that they may improve over time or where I may not be doing things in the optimal way, so if you find a better way to do it, you're probably right.

But I have formatted twenty-plus books with an index in the last year and more before that, so the information in this chapter definitely works.

Okay, then, let's do this. Here is the first page of an index:

Note that entries are listed alphabetically under a single letter of the alphabet with indents for each topic and sub-topic.

If there are two or more pages that you flag consecutively for the same index category, Affinity will automatically show those as pages X-Y as you can see for Color, Apply Specific or Color, Change.

(I swear it used to only do that for three or more pages and I'd have to manually adjust when there were just two pages, but that seems to not be the case in this current version of Affinity I'm working in. So double-check this just in case.)

As we discussed last chapter, I format the master page for my index section in two columns. I find that works well for the labels I give my entries and keeps the index from taking up too much of my document.

Also, the header there, "Index", was added by me on the master page. Your index will insert into your document without any sort of header.

Indexes are managed via the Index studio:

There are also menu options related to indexes under the Text option in the top menu. Go to Text->Index and you'll see the available options there, namely Insert Index Mark, Insert Index, Update Index, and Show Index Marks:

This menu is where I'd get into trouble. I was trying to use the menu option for Insert Index Mark (that shortcut was too complicated for me to actually want to use), but I would accidentally click on Insert Index instead.

Don't be me.

Also note here how Insert Index is grayed out because there's already an index in the document. That's why my workaround worked.

Alright, now that you know where everything is, let's go ahead and walk through how to insert an index into your document.

Here we have a new document where I've pasted in the appendix from my Affinity book and then applied my index master page to the last page and typed in Index into the header section I created:

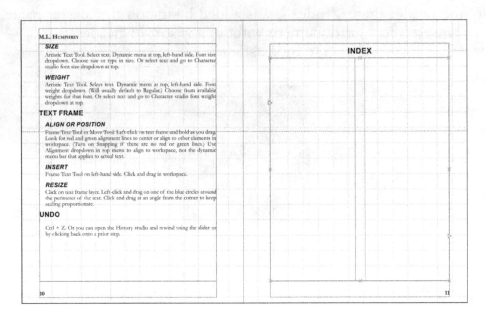

This is a master page I created specifically for use with my index, so there is no text flow from the left-hand page to the right-hand page. Also, the left-hand page has text in a single text frame while the right-hand page is using a text frame that contains two columns.

MARK AN INDEX ENTRY

The first thing I do, as mentioned above, is I flag an entry for my index. It does not matter where that entry is in my document, I just need an entry flagged.

In this case, I'm going to highlight "Text Frame" on the left-hand page and add that to my index.

There are two ways to do this.

The best one is in the Index studio. Click on the little flag for Insert Marker.

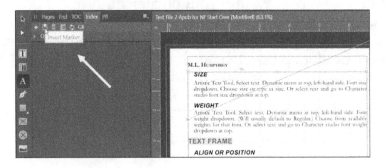

That will open the Insert Index Mark dialogue box and it should also populate the Topic Name field with the text you highlighted.

For me just now it did not populate that field so I had to type it in. But normally you should have something that looks like this:

If the Topic Name is what you want, then click OK. If it is not, change it, and then click OK. If you already have an index mark with the name you want, use the dropdown option to find it.

The other way to mark an entry is through the Text menu. Go to Text->Index and then choose Insert Index Mark from the secondary dropdown. That, too, will open the Insert Index Mark dialogue box.

Or you could use the Ctrl shortcut (Ctrl + Alt +Shift + [ ).

Even though it requires more steps to use the menu option, when Affinity was not showing me my highlighted text in my Topic Name field using the Index studio, that was still working through the menu option. So if you run into that issue you'll have to decide if you'd rather copy and paste or retype your text into the dialogue box, or go through the menu option.

Whichever method you use, when you click OK at the bottom of the dialogue box that will add the text you had in the Topic Name box into your index listing in the Index studio along with a page reference.

You don't have to highlight relevant text to generate an index marker. I sometimes will just click anywhere on a page to set a marker so that I can have my index show that X topic is covered on pages ten through fifteen.

If you don't set a marker on each of those pages it won't show it as a page range. Note also that the page range shown in the index studio is the overall page number in the document, not necessarily the page number that you see on the actual page.

For example, I had front matter in my document, so my index entry shows page 18 even though my formatted document shows that this text was on page 10.

Good news is that despite what it shows in the Index studio, when you insert your index into your document it will show the formatted document page number.

Let's do that now.

INSERT INDEX

Click into your document where you want the index to start and then go to the Index studio and click on the Insert Index option there. It's the third one after the plus sign at the top and looks like a page with some writing on it:

And here you can see that it inserted with page 10 for my text frame entry even though the Index studio shows it on page 18:

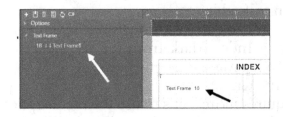

Your other option for inserting an index into your document is the top menu. Go to Text->Index->Insert Index.

UPDATE INDEX

Once you have inserted an index into your document, you can use the Update Index option under Text->Index->Update Index or go to the top of the Index studio and use the option there. It's the one with the circling arrows. Hold your mouse over it and it'll say Update Index.

At least in some versions of Affinity I found that I had to delete the index entries that were already in my document before I could update the index. But just now I wasn't required to do that, so this may be something that's no longer an issue or that only is an issue under certain circumstances.

But basically if you ever try to update your index and it doesn't work, go into your document, delete all of your index entries, and then insert the index again.

PARENT TOPICS

You can get fancier with your index by creating a hierarchy of entries using parent topics.

For example, here in my appendix of quick takes on Affinity I have Align or Position, Insert, and Resize as subcategories under Text Frame.

I want to keep that same hierarchy in my index.

The first step to doing so is making Text Frame into an index entry. We already did that above.

The next step is to take one of the sub-entries I want to put under Text Frame and make an index entry out of it, too. So I'm going to highlight Insert and click to insert an index marker for it.

Affinity auto-populated Topic Name for me. If I clicked on OK right now Insert would be an entry in my index at the same level as Text Frame. But I can click on the dropdown there for Parent Topic and see all of my existing entries in my index:

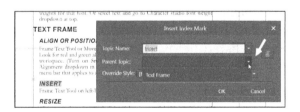

If I choose Text Frame from that dropdown, then Affinity will add Insert as an index entry but it will put that entry under the parent topic, Text Frame.

Here's what the dialogue box looks like after I make that selection:

And here's what my index looks like when I say OK:

See how Insert is indented and listed under Text Frame?

When I then update the index in my document, it is also listed under Text Frame:

Note that both entries appear under T in the index.

REMOVE PAGE NUMBERING FOR PARENT TOPIC

In the screenshot above you can see that both Text Frame and Insert show the page number for the entry. But maybe I don't want Text Frame to have the page numbers listed, too. Maybe I just want it to be a header and only worry about displaying page numbers for the sub-topics like Insert.

In that case, I can go back to the Text Frame entry in my Index studio and delete the page-specific flag I have there under Text Frame. I do so by clicking on that page number entry listed below Text Frame and then using the trash can up top.

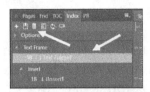

This time when I generate my index the Text Frame entry has no separate page numbering:

MOVE AN EXISTING ENTRY BELOW ANOTHER

Sometimes I will add an entry as a standalone index entry and later change my mind and decide it should be a subtopic instead.

Like here where I have Align or Position as its own entry and then Text Frame as a separate entry.

One way to fix this issue is to left-click and drag the entry you want to be a subtopic onto the entry you want as its parent topic.

The entry you click and drag will be highlighted blue and when you're on top of the parent topic it too will be blue like you can see above. Release the left-click at that point and Affinity should automatically position the entry you moved as a sub-entry to the one you dragged it to. Like this:

You can see that Align or Position is now indented below Text Frame.

Your other option is to right-click on the entry you want to make a sub-topic and choose to Edit Topic from the dropdown menu:

That opens an Edit Topic Index dialogue box that's identical to the dialogue box for inserting a new marker. Add a parent topic there and click OK and it will move the entry for you.

MOVE A SUB-TOPIC ENTRY TO PARENT TOPIC LEVEL

This is also how you can move an entry from being a subtopic back to being a primary topic. Right-click on the entry, choose Edit Topic, and then in the Edit Topic dialogue box click into the Parent Topic field, highlight the text that's there and delete it. You may need to then click back into the Parent Topic field so that no parent topic is selected. When your dialogue box shows your original entry but no value for the parent topic, click on OK.

That will move the entry from underneath its parent topic to its own entry.

MULTIPLE SUB-TOPIC LEVELS

You can nest a topic under more than one topic. For example, let's say I wanted Elements as a parent topic and then I wanted Insert as a sub-topic and then under that I wanted Text Frame, Picture Frame, etc.

I can do that. It works the exact same way. Build from the top down if you're going to do that. So have a topic for Elements and then create a topic for Insert with a parent of Elements. That way when you go to add your topic for Text Frame you'll have a choice in your Parent Topic dropdown that is shown as "Elements, Insert".

That comma between the words is an indicator that the parent topic has multiple levels. It will be listed alphabetically by the highest-level parent topic.

RENAME AN ENTRY

To rename a topic or fix a typo in a topic name, click on the name in the listing in the Index studio and then click on it again until the text is highlighted in blue and can be edited. Type in your updated name. Hit enter.

CROSS-REFERENCES AND ADDING ENTRIES DIRECTLY

Another thing you can do is add a cross-reference in your index.

Let's say that I want to list all of my control commands under one heading but I also want to have people be able to look for something like "Undo" in my index and still find that entry, too.

First, I'm going to add a new entry for Ctrl Commands and I don't want to flag this to one specific entry or page.

I can do so by using the + sign at the top of the Index studio. Clicking on that opens the Add Index Topic dialogue box. I can then type in my text in the Topic Name field and it will add that text as an index entry without a page reference.

Once I have that, I can take an existing index entry, in this case "Undo", and right-click on it. From the dropdown menu I can then choose Add Cross Reference.

This brings up the Add Cross-Reference dialogue box which has a dropdown menu I can select from that contains all of the entries in my index.

I choose Ctrl Commands and choose OK.

Now, this is not going to work yet because I have no actual entries under Ctrl Commands. The index will not update to show a manually-added entry without at least one page reference or sub-topic that has a page reference.

So I now need to create an additional entry for Undo with a parent topic of Ctrl Commands.

Or, if I don't care about listing the page number under my Undo listing, I could just move my existing page reference from Undo up to Ctrl Commands. Which is what I did here:

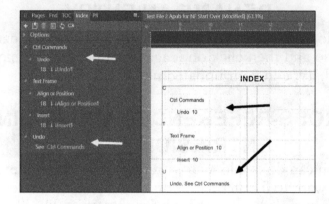

Note how the index under Undo says, "See Ctrl Commands" and there's an entry for Undo under Ctrl Commands with a page number?

You also don't actually have to have overlapping words like that. You can have a cross-reference from Add to Insert, for example, and that would work just as well. All you need is an actual entry under the one being referenced or it won't show in your index.

MANUAL UPDATES

That's the basics of working with an index.

Once your index is inserted into your document it can be edited just like any other text in your document. I will, for example, sometimes combine the entries for letters like U through Z to take up less space.

But remember, just like with the table of contents, because Affinity generates your index for you, if you do make manual edits to your index and then regenerate that index for any reason you will lose those edits.

TEXT STYLE UPDATES

The index does use text styles so you can always edit the formatting of your text and then update that text style if you want to apply that formatting to all of your entries.

OTHER THOUGHTS

What else?

There is a setting there at the top of the Index studio to have it show your index markers for you. I've never used it myself. I basically get everything in the book finalized and then go through from page one to the end and mark things as I see them and then that's it.

Also, sometimes I will use the same sub-topic in a document. So I might have "Insert" under multiple parent categories. This is absolutely doable, but there have been times when Affinity really wanted to use the existing Parent Topic and I needed to click away from choosing that parent topic or get it back to a blank parent topic before I could assign the sub-topic to a new parent topic.

So know it is possible, it just may take a little work to get it right.

That's basically it.

As I mentioned before, you can only have one index in a document.

Nice thing, though, is that if you're merging multiple documents into one, the markers you set in each of those documents will feed into that single index, so you don't have to redo all of that work when you merge documents.

So let's talk about that next, how to merge multiple documents into one. It's another fiddly one but definitely useful to master.

MERGE MULTIPLE BOOKS INTO ONE TITLE

I generally take any series of books I've written and publish it as a collection or omnibus when it's done. So the *Excel Essentials* series, for example, has *Excel for Beginners, Intermediate Excel, 50 Useful Excel Functions,* and *50 More Excel Functions* available as standalone titles but it also has *Excel Essentials* available for purchase. (That thing is a behemoth. It's an inch thick.)

The only time I don't do this is when the book is too massive when combined or when the individual titles were never really meant to be a collection like that. For example, my Easy Excel Essentials series are all meant to be one-off titles for a specific purpose because ideally someone would just buy the Excel Essentials books if they needed more than that.

(Not that people always act in the ways I expect.)

Anyway. Combining multiple books in Affinity is something you will also likely want to do at some point, either for fiction or non-fiction, so it's definitely worth covering. But it can be a lot of fiddly work, so I'm actually going to start with a fiction example which is much simpler to handle and then move on to a non-fiction example after that.

And so I don't forget anything I'm going to work through both examples with real files that need to be combined. It may make things a little longer, but at least there won't be some obvious step I forget.

First up is combining three of my cozy mystery books. I publish these books as standalones but also publish every three books as a collection and right now I have a short story and two of the books for the next collection ready to go so it's a perfect example to use.

I always work off of the file for the first book, so that's step one, open that book in Affinity.

The way I have my collections set up is I have a title page for the collection, a copyright and Also By page for the collection after that, and then a table of contents for the collection.

For my fiction collections I then have a page that has a black and white version of the book cover for the first title and then the copyright information and the text of the first title. I do the same for all of the other books in the collection.

My next step then is to figure out what material I can scavenge from the original file for the first book.

It starts with a title page that I can convert to a title page for the collection.

I can also use the Also By page as-is as well as the pages I have with the book cover, copyright notice, and main body text:

The About the Author at the end will have to go. I'll pull that from the last book I add.

Now that I know what to repurpose, what to keep, and what I need to add I can go to the first page of my document and change the title to the one for the collection.

To do so I click on the Artistic Text Tool (the capital A), go to the first page, and make my changes to the text. Ideally that's all you should have to do.

In my case I had to do more because the text wasn't wrapped around the image, but it needed to be. So that required me to go to the master page and fix that setting.

On the next two-page spread I was able to keep the Also By section on the right-hand page as-is, but I needed to add text for the collection copyright.

I had a choice to either do so on the master page or the actual page in the document. I went ahead and did so in the document itself.

So I clicked and dragged a text frame into place, copied my text from the individual title's copyright page, and pasted it into the frame.

(This has the added benefit of giving me the earliest copyright year I need if I choose to just have one copyright notice, but since I'm leaving the individual copyright notices after their title pages, I'll just do one for the collection.)

I updated the copyright notice to include the word Collection before the word Copyright and XXX'ed out the current ISBN. I'll update that when I'm ready to provide one for the collection, but in the meantime those XXX's should be flagged as a spelling error in preflight so I won't forget to update it.

I also changed the copyright year to this one.

Here we are so far:

In the original document the next page is the page with the cover image, but I need a new page before that with the table of contents for the collection.

I can do that with a right-click and Add Pages selection from the dropdown menu which will bring up the Add Pages dialogue box.

I can either right-click on the Also By page spread and choose to insert the new spread "after" or I can right-click on the book cover image page spread and choose to insert "before". (I could also technically insert anywhere I want and drag the page spread into place, but why add the extra step?)

The master page I use for this is the Simple Title Page, which is the same one I used for page 1.

For now because we don't have the other titles in the document yet, this page is just going to be a placeholder page. Once we have all of the books in I'll need to circle back and either insert a table of contents on this page or manually enter a table of contents. (Not a best practice to manually enter the text, but it looks like that's what I've done with the prior collections for these books. Shame on me.)

Because I know I have that issue I went ahead and at least listed table of contents and the book titles.

After that the next umpteen pages get to be left just as they are because this is the first book and it should be set up to just flow from there.

I do need to check the first page of the first chapter to be sure it starts on page 1, but it should be fine.

And here we are with the rest of the front matter:

Next step is to go to the end of the document and delete anything from the back matter. In my case that's just the final page spread which has my about the author page.

In my fantasy series that would include the character and term listings, because those would need to move to the end of the collection and I'd just use the one from the last book in the series.

Also, sometimes I will have a little "read the next book" note at the end of my last chapter. That text needs to be deleted as well.

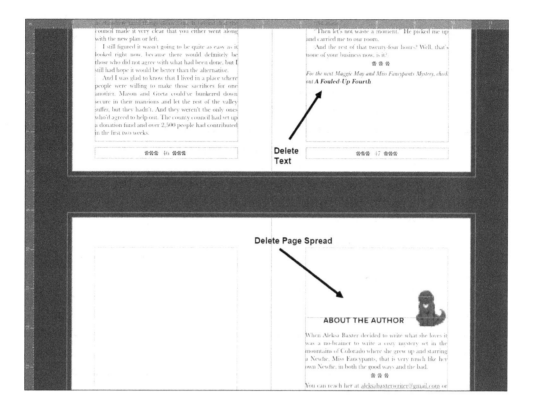

One thing to watch out for when you delete any back matter pages or text at the end of the book is red circles around the text frame. Like this:

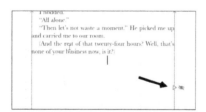

That indicates an overflowing text frame. And what that means in this particular instance is that my "About the Author" text was text that was flowing from my main body text.

Sometimes I set my books up that way, sometimes my about the author text is separate.

If the text were separate I could have deleted those two pages and been done. But because my text is flowing from my main body to that About the Author page the text was not actually deleted when I deleted those two pages.

I have two options for fixing this. I can undo back to before I deleted the pages at the end of the document, delete the text on those pages, and then delete the pages again.

Or I can click at the very end of my main body text and start using the Delete key until I've pulled the text back onto that page where I can then delete it.

I went with the undo option. That way I know I got it all and I'm not stuck in some annoying loop of trying to delete text I can't actually see until I delete it.

When you're done, you want that last page spread to be the end of your first title.

One more thing to do before we move on and bring in the second title. You can technically wait to do this until the end but I'm going to do it now because it'll throw me otherwise.

Right now, because this is a fiction title, my headers are pulling in the book title. But to have this work when it's a collection I need to swap that over to section names and then assign each book to its own section.

To do so, I first go back to the Master Pages section, find any page that has the book title in the header and swap that out for the Section Name field.

In this case I have the Chapter Start and Text master page as well as the Text and Text master page to fix.

Remember you do this by highlighting the book title, deleting it, and then going to Text->Insert->Fields->Section Name.

Once that's done, go to the first page of Chapter 1, right-click, Start New Section, and name that section for the first title in your collection.

Now it's time to bring in the next book.

This is where it gets wacky. Because even though in a standalone title the first page starts on the right-hand side, that's not how it works when you add that file onto the end of another one.

Affinity also does not treat that first page spread as a two-page spread. Which means that unless you prep your file properly the first page of the next book will come in on the left-hand side and all of your pages will be off by one. Everything that should be on the right will be on the left, and vice versa.

To not have this problem, what I'm going to do is go to the end of my current document and insert a two-page spread.

I want one that has a blank left-hand page. It really doesn't matter which one I choose as long as that left-hand page is blank.

Next, I'm going to right-click on the right-hand page of that spread and delete that right-hand page.

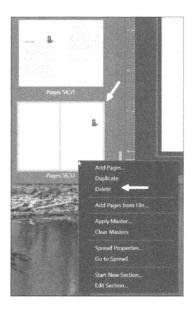

Note that I am only deleting the right-hand page. See that the blue outline is only around that page, not the page spread.

Doing this leaves me with a document that has a blank page at the end on the left-hand side. Which means when I bring in my next file, the next place to put a page will be on the right-hand side and all of my pages will be in the appropriate place.

To do that, I right-click on that last page and choose Add Pages from File from the dropdown:

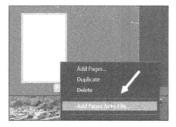

That will open a dialogue box where I can navigate to the second book file and choose Open. At that point Affinity will show the Add Pages dialogue box.

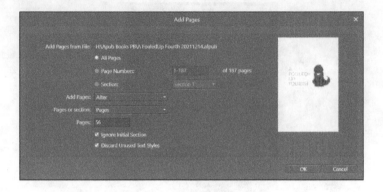

I want All Pages, After, Pages, and my last page number which in this case is 56.

I tried this both with and without Ignore Initial Section checked and it didn't make any difference that I could see.

For some odd reason it brought my first page in without text, but since we're going to delete it, that's fine.

I now have three page spreads at the beginning of my second title that look like this:

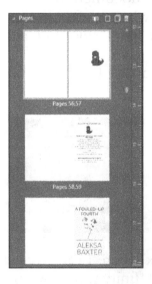

The page there at the top with the blue outline is the last page from our first file that we inserted. The page next to it is the title page for my second title and then the rest of the pages you see are the ones that flow from there.

Every once in a while when you try to bring in another book you may run into a situation where there is an Imported Text Styles dialogue box that appears. This won't always happen, but it definitely can. That generally means there's some sort of conflict or overlap between the styles used in the two documents.

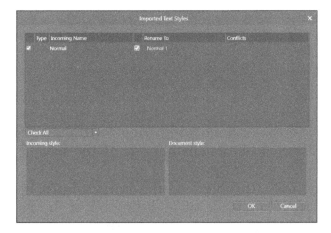

For example here I probably for some reason have a style in each file named Normal. If I don't want to change any of my text formatting I can just click the Rename To box and that will keep both text styles in the document and rename the one for the imported file to Normal 1 so the two styles don't have the same name anymore.

That's usually what I do. I can then scan the document later for any big differences and fix them at that point with a find and replace for text style or by manually applying the text style I want. But at the import stage I like to just leave things alone.

Okay, back to our file with the newly-imported second book.

Because this is the second title in the collection I don't need the same front matter. I can have this section start with the book cover, which means I can delete the first two page spreads, the one with the title page and the one with the also by text.

Next, I need to set a section start on the page for chapter 1 of this second book and give that section the book's name. I also want to make sure to continue numbering because you don't start page numbering over with a collection:

But in this case I need to continue numbering for the prior section, too, which covers the two blank pages before chapter one of the second book starts as well as the page with the book cover image.

You can see that was a problem in the image above because Section 4 is showing 1-3 in the right-hand side of its listing but it should be showing 48-50 because it should be continuing the numbering of the prior section like Section 5 is currently doing. (Section 5 shows page 59-239 on the left-hand side which represent the overall pages in the document contained in the section but 4-184 on the right-hand side because it is continuing the page numbering from Section 4.)

If that sounds confusing, don't worry about it. You'll see in the document itself that your numbers are off and know you need to fix them. You can even save that for the very end if you want when you scan through the whole thing.

Okay.

Next step is to go to the end of the newly-merged document and delete any back matter. Keep going through those steps for each book you want to include until you reach the last one.

When you reach the final file, don't delete the back matter like you did with the other files you brought in. Instead, see which parts of the back matter to keep. In this case I just have an about the author page, so that definitely stays.

The next step is to do a scan through and review to make sure everything landed where it should, that your page numbers are continuous from the first title through, and that your headers reflect the correct book.

You can generate a PDF at this point and review that or just scroll up and down and view the pages on your screen. If you do export to PDF this is a good time to export as All Spreads because then the pages will export as a pair with the left-hand page on the left-hand side and the right-hand page on the right-hand side of the spread so it's easier to review that the content is on the correct side of the page.

(You can't submit an All Spreads export to KDP or IngramSpark, but it is handy for document review.)

The final step is the table of contents. Best to finalize that when everything else in the document is as it should be.

In this case, I'd been doing these manually which is not a best practice. What I can do instead since I don't have a title page to pull my titles from, is insert a text frame layer behind the cover images for each of my titles. That will hide that layer during the export. I can then add my title to that hidden text frame, assign a book title text style to it, and use that book title style to generate my table of contents.

That works. Affinity generates a table of contents for me, shows the start page for each book as the page with the cover image on it, and on those cover image pages I don't see the text in that hidden text frame.

Done. Now on to the harder example, a non-fiction collection.

* * *

I'm going to create a collection using the first three Affinity books.

First step then is to open *Affinity Publisher for Fiction Layouts*.

The front matter we want for the collection is going to be very similar to that we had for fiction.

I want a collection title page, collection copyright, an also by page, an overarching table of contents and then an individual book title page, individual book copyright page, individual book table of contents, and individual book content.

At the end I want any relevant appendix that applies across the books as well as an index for all the titles.

To make this happen, I need to insert two new page spreads, one for the first book's title page and one for the overarching table of contents. Since they use different master page layouts I inserted them one at a time but I could have inserted them both at once and then just changed the master page style for one or the other.

My next step is to copy the text from the first page, which contains my original title page text, and paste that into my newly-inserted master page that will be for the first book's title page.

I do it this way, because that first page spread is a little funky since it's only a right-hand page and I don't want to deal with whatever complications inserting a master page at the start might create. So better to copy and paste the text from that page and then type over the existing text on that first page to create my collection title page.

That's what I do next.

I do the copyright notice after that. In this case, I copy the copyright text for the individual title and paste it into an inserted text frame that I place right before the page for the collection table of contents. I then edit that copyright notice to pertain to the collection.

For now we're going to leave the table of contents page empty.

So here are our first five pages. We have the collection title page, the collection copyright, the also by, a blank page, and then the table of contents for the collection:

After those five pages, we have the beginning of the first book which contains its title page, copyright notice, and table of contents:

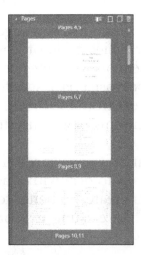

So far this is very similar to what we did for the cozy mystery collection, but now things change.

First, I do not have to create any sections this time. That's because I already had sections since I was using chapter titles for my headers.

Second, this book has its own table of contents so that's going to require some adjustments.

Look at the last four items that are currently in that table of contents:

There are two appendices, an index, and an about the author page. All of those should be part of the collection, not part of this individual title. Which means this table of contents will need updated at some point after we delete those sections.

Also, to make my life difficult, the quick takes in this first book here are not the same as the ones for the ads and book covers titles which are books two and three in the collection. Very different tasks involved between print formatting and image manipulation.

So I need to make a choice. Do I integrate the two quick takes appendices into one large quick takes appendix? Or keep them separate?

I think I'm going to try to keep them separate. For now, though, I can just delete this.

So my next step is to go to the end of the present document and delete those four sections. I want to delete the contents of the index, though, before I delete the pages it is on.

To do so, I go to the index section, click into that text frame with my index contents, use Ctrl + A to select all of my index entries, and then use the Delete key.

I also need to individually delete the "Index" text at the top of that page. Otherwise it may end up somewhere weird when I delete that page.

Now I can delete all of the back matter pages.

I end up with a final page on the left-hand side that has text on it. Which means I need a blank page on the right-hand side to match that page as well as one additional blank page by itself on the left-hand side after that.

When I try to apply a text and no text master page to that last page to add my right-hand blank page, nothing happens. It just stays a single standalone page.

If I had a no text and no text master page, I could just insert it here, but I don't.

What I can do, though, is insert a no text and chapter start master page, and then go to the newly orphaned last page that is a chapter start page and change its assigned master page style to a no text and text master page style.

It's an awkward way for me to get two blank pages in a row like that, but it does seem to work.

Now that I have that blank left-hand page by itself I can bring in the second book using the Add Pages from File option and know that the pages will fall where they should.

This one had a lot of Imported Text Styles it wanted to show me:

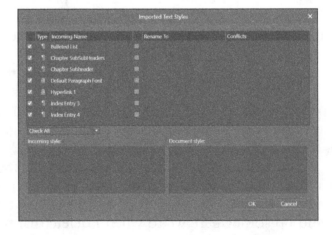

But since there are no conflicts listed, I'm just going to click on OK. That means both documents will use the same text styles.

Each one should be the same style with the same formatting, and they came in fine as far as I can tell right now.

I tested it with a quick search for any text with one of the styles using the Find option and then scrolled down until I found an image in that same section to confirm it didn't accidentally shift the text due to a formatting change.

It looks like there was no impact. And there really shouldn't have been because I created book two using the file from book one. (I am lazy so I just open the last book in the series, delete the main body content from that last book, and then drop in the next book's content when I'm ready to do the next book in a series.) It would only be a problem if I'd for some reason changed that style in book two. But then Affinity should've told me there was a conflict, which it did not.

(Always do a final pass of your document, though.)

Okay.

Next I need to move the copyright notice for this book to the page spread with the table of contents specific to book two and then I can delete the Also By page spread.

After that, I can go to the end of the newly-merged document and delete book two's back matter.

And that crashed my file.

If that happens to you, don't panic. Open Affinity again and you should see a message like this:

I always say Yes.

Now you get to find out how much you lost and also, if you're me, cuss at yourself for not saving a version of the file yet.

So first step is to save the file under the name you actually wanted to use for it if you're me.

Second step is to see what you lost. Fortunately, my answer is nothing. It saved right up until the pages I tried to delete that it didn't like me deleting. Which is usually the case with Affinity. I have definitely had it crash on me, but do not recall losing a significant amount of edits when that happened.

Which leaves us with a choice to make.

Do we assume the crash was a one-off error and try to delete those same pages again, possibly risking crashing the program a second time? Or do we take a more measured approach?

I'm going to assume it's my index giving me issues, which means it'll do it again.

So I'm going to do a Ctrl + A in my index section and delete the text of the index before I try to delete my pages.

This time it did not crash. Yay!

Now that those pages are gone I can add two blank pages at the end like I did before and insert my final file. (For now. In reality this book I'm writing right now will be the final file. But we'll pretend.)

This time I did have a conflict in the Imported Text Styles:

I can leave it like this and it will change the bulleted list style for one of the two books, or I can check that Rename To box and let it bring the bulleted list style used in the third book as a new style.

I'm going to check the box. I have too many images in these books to mess up any of my spacing. (You'll understand better why that's an issue for me when we cover image placement in the next chapter.)

Okay.

Same process with the front matter. Move the copyright notice, delete the also by page.

Now we have to deal with the Appendices and the Index. This is the last table of contents in the document, so if we don't change the text style assigned to the Appendix, the Index, and the About the Author sections to something different from our chapter titles, then the table of contents for book three will include them like it is currently:

We don't want that.

So let's go to the Appendix now. We have a choice to make. We can continue to have the Appendix formatted the exact same way as before but just assign it a new style name. Or we can change the formatting and assign that its own name.

I'm lazy, so I'm going to just create a new style but not make any formatting changes. Which means we can click onto the Appendix title row and then go up to the Text Style dropdown menu and choose New Style from there and give the text style its own name.

It is unchanged and identical looking to the chapter style, but now we can differentiate the two for table of contents purposes.

Next I need to go through and apply that new style to any other back matter headers I have. Easy enough.

And now the annoying bits.

First, I have two appendices from the first book that I need to bring back in. (Let me pause to save my file real quick…)

The first of those appendices was eight pages long. I'm going to click onto the last main page of my third book and insert eight pages with a text and text master page format using the Add Pages option in the dropdown menu.

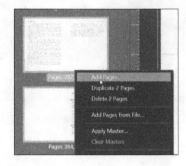

Once the pages are inserted I can go to the first set of inserted pages and change the master page format to a no text and section start master page.

I'm now going to go back to the first file, copy the text for that first Appendix and paste the text into this page. The text does not automatically flow to the next page, but good news is it also doesn't end up back in the main body of my third book.

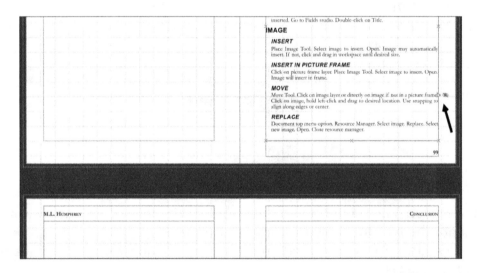

Because I have content past this inserted section, I can't have Affinity auto-flow the appendix text for me. So I need to click on that red triangle and then click in my text frame on the left-hand side frame on the next page and keep doing that for all of the pages of this appendix to get the text to flow through.

After I've done that I can go back to the appendix header, apply my new back matter text style, and also change the name since I'm going to have two quick takes appendices.

I can now change the name for the second quick takes appendix as well, making it Appendix B and specific to images.

I decided to put the other appendix from the first book behind the quick takes appendices. It's the same process of adding pages for the text and then bringing in the text and flowing it through.

Now it's time to tackle the Index.

But, actually, it isn't. Because I want my page numbers behaving before I do this and I don't think they are. Actually, I know they aren't. Not unless three books plus appendices are 118 total pages.

To figure out where my issue is, I right-click on a page spread in the Pages studio and choose Edit Section to bring up the Section Manager. Once I have the Section Manager open I can go through my sections after that first introduction chapter and see where I need to tell Affinity to continue numbering.

It sounds worse than it is because the only sections that should be giving me a problem are the title page or table of contents or introduction pages for each book. It won't be every single section that needs updating since those were already set up appropriately when I created the original books.

While I'm at it, I should assign sections to the two appendices I pasted into the document manually.

Okay, so once that's done and I'm comfortable that the page numbering throughout the whole document is working properly (238 pages is much more like it), I can finally tackle the Index. Here's the first page:

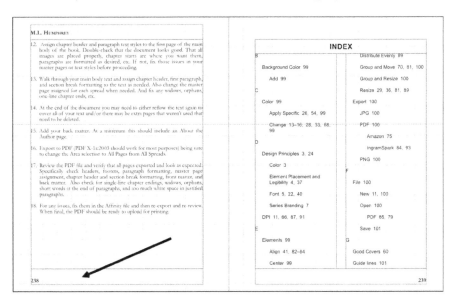

You can see that there are already entries there. But I'm not sure this index is pulling in entries from all three books.

To be sure, I need to refresh the index. Let me see if the Update option will work.

I go to the Index studio and click on the arrows at the top for Update and, yes, it worked. (If that didn't work I would've just deleted the index entries I could see in the document and then used the Insert option instead.)

Because this is now an index with entries for three books instead of one, I have more text than available space as you can see from the red arrows around the text frames:

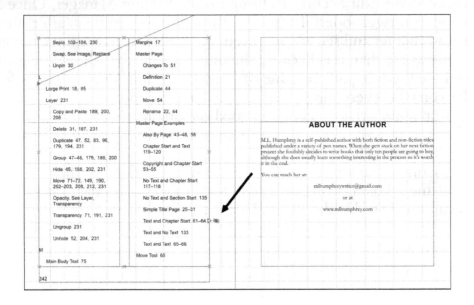

That means I need to go back to the Pages studio, insert some new pages between that index page and my about the author page, assign the proper master pages to them, and then flow my text to get the whole index visible.

And I realized as I did that I must've missed one "continue numbering" option with my pages because I have 414 pages showing on the left-hand side in the Pages studio but my document is only showing 250 or so pages.

So I have to fix that, too, and then update the index one more time. Fortunately, it's pretty easy to know when you've messed up and find the fix. Unfortunately, I don't think I've ever done one of these books where there wasn't something that I missed the first time through.

It happens, so prepare for that and check, recheck, and check again.

The easiest way to find where that happened is to scroll back through the pages in my workspace until I see a page 1. My Pages studio will roughly keep pace as I do so, which means when I get to that point I can then right-click on the correct page spread in the Pages studio, Edit Section, and update that section to continue numbering.

Here's the culprit. I have a page 1 in my layout but it's page 167 of my overall document:

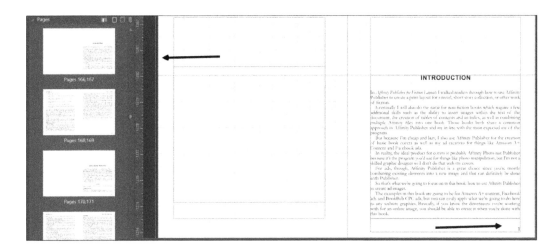

So time to right-click, Edit Section, and fix it. Just make sure that you're making your changes to that actual section and not a different one. (Like I almost did just now…)

Finally it's time to deal with our tables of contents. Remember, we have four of them—the overarching one that will list our book titles and back matter and then the three individual ones that will list the chapters for each book.

It's probably easier to do the back three before we do the front one, but we can also take care of a few things along the way that will help with the main table of contents.

So I'm going to go back to the start of the document and scroll down until I see my first title page that isn't the collection title page. I click on that title and note the text style used. In my case it's Book Title. I'll need that later for my main table of contents.

I keep going to the next page which has the table of contents for this specific book. I click into the document where the TOC text is and then look at the TOC studio.

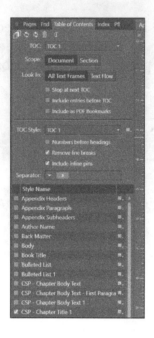

(Now's when I hope I didn't do a lot of manual formatting to any of my tables of contents.)

The first thing I need to do for this table of contents is check the "Stop at next TOC" box. That's going to update my table of contents so that it stops pulling entries when it reaches book two.

The next thing I need to do is see if it looks okay now. How's the formatting? Any weird page-numbering issues? Any weird text entries? Any text overflow? There shouldn't be, but if it turns out I manually adjusted things, there could be.

Also, I need to make sure that the last entry in this table of contents is the last chapter in this particular book and that it's no longer pulling in the appendices, about the author, or other back matter sections.

(Sometimes even though you deleted the pages that had those sections on them the headers can get caught somewhere in the ether and be hanging out behind the scenes and they'll show up in your table of contents entries. This usually happens if the text flowed from the last chapter straight into the back matter instead of those being completely separate sections of your document.)

So let's look:

All good. The last entry listed is the Conclusion just as it should be.

On to the next.

I locate the next table of contents, click into it, change the TOC dropdown to TOC 2 in the Table of Contents studio, check the box for stop at next TOC, and then verify that it too looks okay.

Here's that dropdown:

If you don't change the dropdown to the next TOC even though you're clicked onto it all of the settings will still be for that first table of contents, and when you click on Update it will update the first table of contents not the one you're clicked on.

(Ask me how I know…)

This one looks good, too, so on to the third one. Same process.

Except when I updated my third table of contents my first table of contents pulled in the entries from my second table of contents and wouldn't refresh to get rid of them.

I obviously could've been messing something up somewhere, but the only solution I found that worked was to delete that first table of contents and re-insert it. Of course, that required me to reformat my table of content entries because it was a new table of contents.

Good times.

Okay. Once you've sorted your interior tables of contents, it's time to insert the main, overarching table of contents.

I go back to that blank fifth page of my document, click into the text frame for where I want to insert the table of contents, and then go to the Table of Contents studio and click on the Insert option:

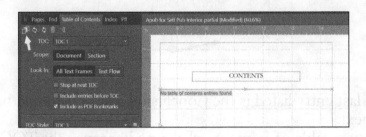

Hopefully it defaults to no entries found like this one did so you can just go check the boxes for the styles you need. I know that I want to use Book Title and Back Matter to flag my entries based on what I noted down previously. When I do that I get this result:

That is very ugly.

And it's going to require some manual adjustment on my part to fix because I had line breaks on my title pages. But let's save that for last.

First, I need to go back to the Tables of Contents studio and for each style I need to tell it to include page numbers.

Next, I need to highlight one of the lines of text and change the formatting to what I want. I'm going to use Garamond, 16 pt, small caps. I update the text style so all of the entries for that style update and then go do the same for the other entries under the second text style.

Which gets me this:

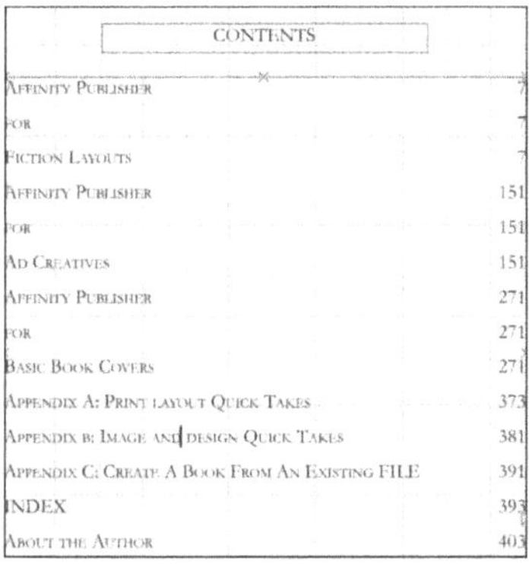

CONTENTS

I now have two choices. I can go to the title pages for each book and remove those line breaks and just let the text flow as it will. That will let this table of contents update automatically without needing manual adjustments. Or I can remove those line breaks here on the page, but the next time I update this table of contents I'll have to fix it again. (And I know I'll have to update the table of contents again because I still need to add in this book I'm writing right now.)

Also, I always forget about the difference in appearance between INDEX and Index when I'm using small caps. See how that stands out atrociously? Same with the word FILE.

So I need to go adjust that text, too, to make it upper and lower case.

I went to that first title page, removed the line breaks, and decided it worked just fine so did that to the other two and then made my edits to file and index and here we go:

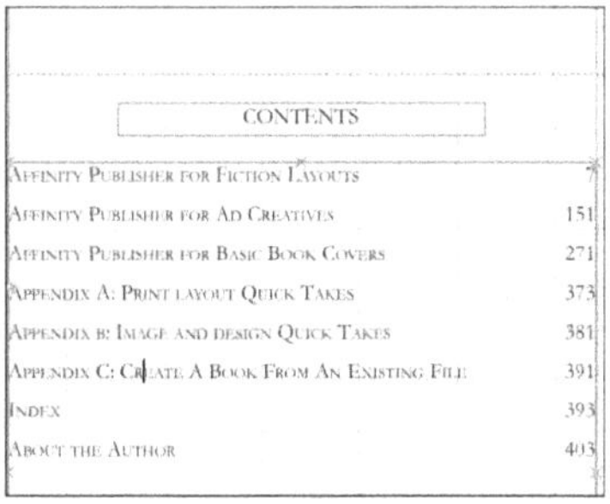

CONTENTS

Much, much better.

Although that B in Appendix B still needs fixed. Looks like it's lower-case right now.

And I might want to change my formatting so that the back matter is somehow set apart from the three main book titles, but for now, we're good.

If this were the final version of this book I'd now need to generate my PDF and scan through the whole thing making sure that page starts fall where they should and that all images imported properly and that nothing moved around.

I'd also want to see that my headers still make sense and double-check my page numbering.

It's a lot of work to merge non-fiction books in Affinity, but it's a helluva lot better to do it this way than have to go through and re-place 100+ images per book and add markers for a new index.

Speaking of images, let's talk about image placement and adjustment next.

IMAGE PLACEMENT

I saved image placement for last because I wanted to be sure I delivered value before diving in on this topic.

Now, don't get me wrong, I have a lot of experience placing images in Affinity documents. Each of these books has around a hundred different screenshots and at this point I've done over a dozen image-heavy books between the Excel, Word, Access, PowerPoint, and Affinity titles.

And, yes, they have turned out okay. If you're reading this in print and you've reached this point then I have to assume you didn't yet throw the book across the room because you couldn't read the images.

But. (There's always a but.) I don't think that the way I place images in Affinity is the way you're really supposed to do it.

Because I use picture frames to place my images. I did this initially because I wanted every image I placed to have a border around it and that was the easiest way I could find to make that happen. Also, I found it easier to center my images using a picture frame.

It does also let me control which part of an image is visible on the page, but that's generally not something that's an issue since I want the images I use in the print version and the ebook version to be the same. I think maybe half a dozen times I've not shown the full image in the print version simply because it wasn't truly necessary and making the image smaller helped with formatting the page.

So I like using picture frames and will continue to do so.

The issue with my approach is that the images I insert are not anchored to the text around them. So if you were to go into one of my books and add a new paragraph at the start of a chapter, all of the text would move, but the images wouldn't. The images are fixed to that location on that page where I placed them.

Since I bring in a final product for formatting in Affinity, this isn't something that causes me a problem. But if you're going to be doing a lot of editing within the file after you place your images, then you may not want to use my approach.

You can instead pin an image to text in your document and when that text moves it will take the image along with it.

I suspect that's probably the better approach. I'm just a person who finds something that works "good enough" for me and then moves forward and the picture frame approach was that solution.

I'll cover both here, though. And I will show you how to place a border directly on your image and use the pinning settings to center it. So really the only difference between the two when we're done will be if you want to crop out part of a larger image.

Also, you'll notice in my books that I always have the image on its own line, but we'll cover how to flow text around an image instead if that's what you prefer.

Okay. Now that the disclaimers are done, let's dive in.

IMAGE QUALITY

The first topic we need to cover does not actually involve using Affinity. And that is image quality.

For print you want all of your images in your book to be 300 DPI or higher for grayscale and 600 DPI for pure black and white images (like line drawings).

And for black and white print books your color should be set to be grayscale. For IngramSpark they recommended Gray/8 last time I checked.

If you upload a file to IngramSpark that has images in it that are not at least 300 DPI (they use ppi in their guidelines but they're basically the same), they will give you an alert message.

You can override the message and they will still publish your book, but the images in your book may be blurry. Or at least blurrier than they need to be.

I will confess that the first *Excel for Beginners* edition I ever published had images that were under 300 DPI. They were still legible, but they were not as crisp as in later editions.

It was actually trying to solve this issue that led me to using Affinity, because Affinity will tell me when my images are not a high enough DPI, which is so so nice to have.

It turned out I had a multi-pronged problem. One was that I was using Word which by default compresses images. Two was that the built-in Save As PDF feature in Word also did something behind the scenes that reduced image quality, so I had to have the Adobe website convert my files for me instead. And the third prong of my problem was that I didn't have a good enough monitor to take the pictures in the first place.

It turns out that the default monitor on most laptops is simply not a high enough resolution to take images that you can use in a print book. At least, not if you want them to be any sort of reasonable size. I'd had hopes that I could connect to my TV and do it that way, but it turns out the resolution on a big television is not necessarily higher than a laptop screen.

Ultimately I had to buy a monitor that was the highest resolution I could find and that finally let me have 300 DPI images that were also large enough for a print book. (With ebooks this is not an issue because ebooks tend to only require 72 DPI or higher. That's also why you can't see this issue until you print out your images.)

Now, there are tricks you can play to make an image 300 DPI, but don't. If you take an initially 100 DPI image and make it 300 DPI it will still be just as blurry as when it was 100 DPI.

Your best bet for a good image is to take it with a high quality monitor or camera to begin with.

Okay, now that we've covered that. Let's walk through placing some images.

IMAGE PLACEMENT

While I'm writing my first draft I take my screenshots and I put a note in the text to indicate that there's an image that needs to be inserted at that spot.

This means when I paste in my text to Affinity I can then work through the document, formatting my text and placing my images as I go.

Here, for example, is the beginning of a chapter of the Affinity for covers book:

You can see that I need to insert three images here. Images 3, 4, and 5.

(I also try to number the images as I go through so that they're in order in the file where I save them, but I almost invariably end up adding text somewhere in the document and then end up with images numbered things like 3a, 3b, 3c etc. to keep them in order.)

So once I've formatted that text at the start of the chapter my next step is to insert a picture frame. I go to the left-hand menu, click on the Picture Frame Rectangle Tool, and then place a rectangle in my document at about the place where I have my note that an image should be inserted.

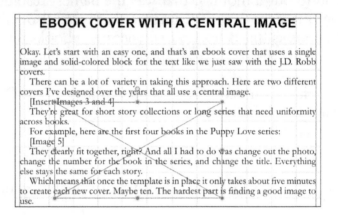

You can see that the frame when I insert it is on top of my text. I don't want that, so what I then do is go to the menu up top and click on the Show Text Wrap Settings option and choose Jump from the Wrap Style.

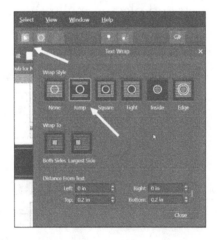

If you didn't want your image to be on its own line, this is where you could choose square or tight instead and have the text wrap either on both sides or the largest side. But as you've seen in the print version of this book and as I mentioned before, I always use jump so the image is by itself, like this:

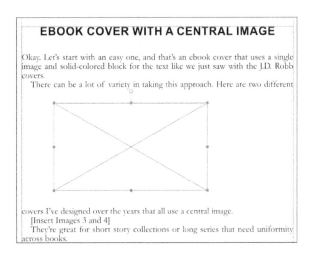

You can see that it's not quite in the correct place. It needs to move down a bit, and I could click and drag on that frame and pull it down right now so that the line of text that ends with "a central image" is above the frame, but I'm not going to.

First I want to bring in my picture, because right now I have no idea what the actual size of the image I'm bringing in is. This picture frame is not going to stay this size. And if I'm going to have to position the frame to center it when I'm done placing the image, I might as well wait to move the picture frame down until then.

Okay. So next step is to go to the Place Image Tool and bring that image in.

Usually when I bring an image in it tries to place it in the picture frame, but I accidentally changed my settings recently so that my images have started coming in at the top left of the page and at the DPI for my document, in this case 300. Which means I insert the image and then can't see it anywhere on the page.

If this happens to you, the way to find the image is to go to your Layers studio, expand the picture frame layer, and click on the image layer below it. That should place a blue border around the image like you're seeing here in the top left corner of the page spread:

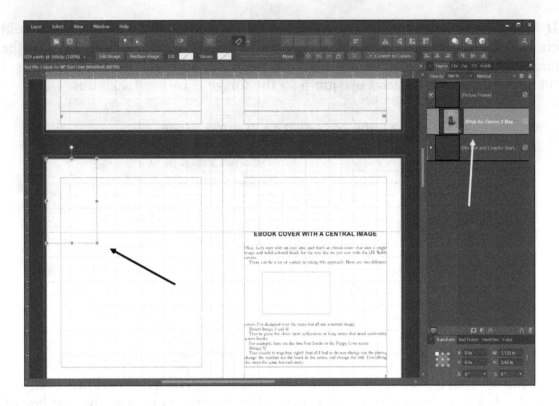

The image itself is not visible because it's inserted in a picture frame but no part of the image overlaps with the picture frame right now.

If clicking on the image layer doesn't work to make its outline visible, then go to the Transform studio and change the X or Y value for the layer to bring it to where the picture frame is or at least within the perimeter of your canvas.

Since I can see it, I click and drag it into place in the picture frame.

As I mentioned above, the nice thing about the image importing this way is that Affinity brings it in at my specified minimum DPI. That can be very helpful if you have smaller images that you're working with because you will know that the image you imported cannot be bigger than that imported size without dropping below your desired DPI.

You can also be assured that if you make that image smaller, it will still be okay. Here, for example, the image came into my picture frame at 300 DPI, but I don't need it to be that big. See that blue outline and how much space it takes up:

You can always see the image DPI in the Resource Manager:

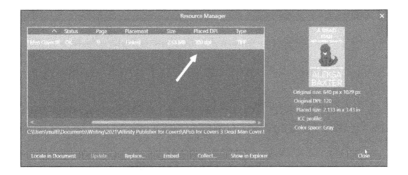

To adjust the image size, I use the Transform studio. That lets me be certain that I'll keep the image proportionate as I change its size.

To do so, I click on the image layer in the Layers studio and then go to the Transform studio and click on the Lock Aspect Ratio setting to the right of the W and H values.

I then change either W or H to what I want. If I drew the picture frame at the approximate size I wanted to use already I can use that H value or I can just guess based on the current size of the image in the document and how much I want to make the image smaller

As you decrease your image size, the DPI will go up. See here where my DPI is now 512:

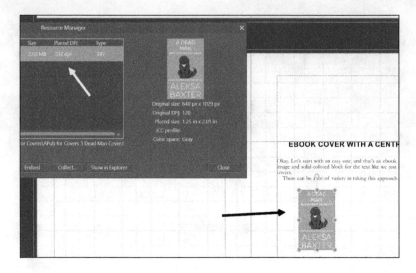

Now that the image is the size I want it to be, I need to also change my picture frame to match.

To do so, click on the picture frame layer, go to the dynamic menu up top, and click on the Size Frame to Content option.

That will both align the frame with the image and make them the same size.

Once you have your image sized and aligned inside your picture frame, it's time to position the frame relative to the text.

Go to the Layers studio and click onto the picture frame layer. Next, click onto the picture frame in your document and drag the image and frame into place.

Always be certain that you are positioning the picture frame layer not the image layer. The image moves with the frame so positioning the picture frame places them both. But if you position the image it will leave the picture frame behind and you'll then have to get the image centered on the frame once more before you position the frame.

In my case, I need to drag the frame down a little to move that one line of text up. I also want it centered.

When centering an image in a book you need to make sure that you use the correct center line, because Affinity will show you two of them. One line centers the image across the entire page, which includes the uneven margins, and one centers the image within the text frame.

You want to center within the text frame.

I believe that correct center line is always going to be the outer line, but I just do it visually. One center line looks right, one does not. This one looks right to me, so I'm done:

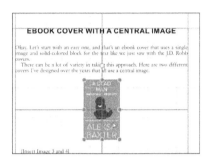

All I need to do now is delete the text that told me to insert my image. (We're ignoring for the moment the fact that I was supposed to insert two images here on this line. If I'd actually done that I would have had to insert both images, group them, and then center the group.)

Okay. I will also often format the next paragraph to remove the indent. Whether you do or not is a style preference, just be consistent throughout that title whichever choice you make.

So I inserted my first image and it's now time to insert the next one, but we have an issue. Look here:

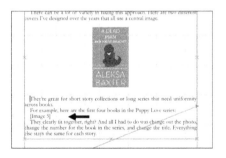

There is no way that image five, whatever it is, will fit at the bottom of this page. Not happening. But because we're using picture frames for this Affinity isn't going to automatically adjust my text placement for me either.

I need to tell Affinity to move all of the text below "Puppy Love series:" to the next page. I do this by inserting a Frame Break using Text->Insert->Breaks->Frame Break right after that colon.

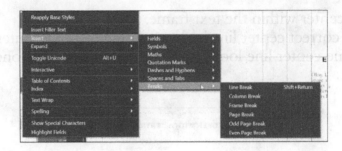

A frame break pushes all of the text below that point to the next text frame, which in this case is also on the next page.

It also seems to insert an actual line as well. So if that happens to you, just delete it.

Now I can place my image at the top of the next page and have all of the text that should be after that image where it belongs.

With that problem solved, it's the same process again for this image. Add my picture frame. Put my image in the picture frame. Resize the image. Resize the frame to match. Move the image so they're overlapped. Move the picture frame into position. Delete the note. Done.

Now I want to walk you through how to change that import setting for the picture frame so that the image comes right into the frame.

First step is to add the picture frame. That changes the dynamic menu up top to the one for the picture frame and gives us a Properties option.

Clicking on Properties gives me a series of choices about how I bring in an image into my frame.

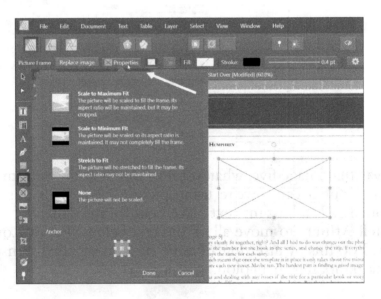

Right now it's set to just anchor in the top left corner of the page. (You can see that the little box in the anchor section that's in the top left-corner is a bright white compared to the others which are gray.)

Interestingly enough, once I fixed this appearance I couldn't replicate it, so it could've been some weird bug I triggered where there was no option selected up top, but I'm just going to continue as if that's a possible option.

To get the picture to come into the picture frame directly you need to choose one of the four options above that.

For what we're doing here, we do NOT want to use Stretch To Fit because it will skew the image by stretching it to the height and width of the picture frame.

Scale To Maximum Fit will try to fit the image to either the width or height of the frame, whichever creates the maximum fit. This means part of the image will fall outside of the frame.

Here that is. See how it came in inside the picture frame and matched the height of the frame but the image is wider than you can see here?

If we use this option, that means we need to be much more careful about the DPI because I don't know what DPI this image is now. I told Affinity to worry about putting the image in the frame, not to worry about the DPI.

Let's go to the Resource Manager to see:

And, yep, see, that's a problem. We need a DPI of 300 or more, but because I asked Affinity to scale to my randomly-drawn picture frame, the image came in at 260 DPI.

Even if this image looked like it was the size I want, it would need to be smaller to get that DPI over 300.

Scale To Minimum Fit tries to fit the image into the frame entirely which means that there will likely be space around the top, bottom, or edge but the image will be fully visible. So in this example the image would have a lot of space probably on the top.

It also is going to have similar issues with DPI. We won't know until we check what the image DPI is.

The final option there, None, does not try to fit the image to the picture frame. It simply brings the image into the frame. And, from what I can tell, does so at the DPI set in your document. That's the one I like for this purpose.

(I should add that I found it better to set my document DPI to 305 instead of 300 because every so often an imported image showed in the Resource Manager with a DPI of 299 after it imported.)

* * *

Now let me show you how to bring in an image without using a picture frame.

First, click where the image should go. Next, go straight to the Place Image Tool, click on it and select your image. The image should come in as-is on top of your text:

(See the text peeking out along the edges of that image there?)

When an image imports like this, the image is "anchored" to where you clicked when you inserted it:

It's a little hard to see, but there's a blue line connecting that image to the spot I clicked when I inserted the image and there's a blue dot at that location to mark the spot.

I tell Affinity to jump the image just like we did with the picture frame, and I get this:

You can better see the anchor now, right? But the text is no longer behind the image like it was before.

Now. The main differences between this approach and the one I showed you with picture frames is that the image will move with the text.

So here I inserted a page and half worth of enters to move the text to the next page, and the image went with that text:

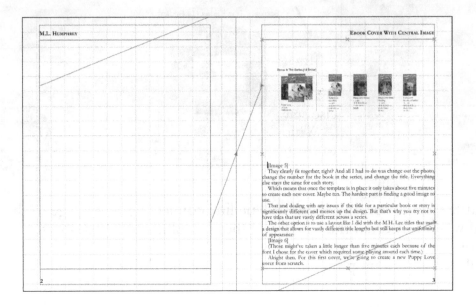

Had I done the same thing with this image in a picture frame, the picture frame would not have moved at all. It would still be in that top left corner of the prior page, regardless of where the text it belonged with went.

So directly inserting an image ensures that the image will stay with its text.

But you have to be careful what text you anchor the image to. I just deleted that text about image 5 and it took the image with it. Always anchor to the text above or below where you want to insert your image. Sometimes the text above will be the better choice, sometimes the text below. (At least in my experience when I was still trying to work with pinned images.)

To work with positioning the image, you need to use the Pinning studio. I don't keep that open, but here it is:

There are two types of images, floating and inline.

You're generally going to want a floating image. Inline images appear to be more for, say, a drop cap. Affinity's help text says that inline images are treated like a character within the text.

The image I pinned above was a floating image. In the Float tab, the Horizontal Align setting will let you align the image to the left, center, or right of the text frame or page. You want Inside Center for Frame to center in the text fame.

Vertical Align will change the vertical positioning of the image relative to the pin.

The horizontal and vertical offset values are where you can specify the exact position of the image relative to where it's pinned.

To unpin an image, click on unpin. That will let you manually move the image around.

To repin the image just click on Float or Inline in the Pinning dialogue box.

You can left-click and drag a pin in your text to anchor the image to different text.

Affinity's help instructions actually have you insert the image first and then pin it. To do that, don't click anywhere in the text first, just place the image and then click on the image and use the Pinning studio to pin it.

You can also pin an image using the menu option at the top that appears when you have an image selected as shown here:

For full position control, though, you need the pinning studio open.

To place a border around an image like this, change the settings for Stroke while the image is selected. Here, for example, I've placed a dark black border around the image:

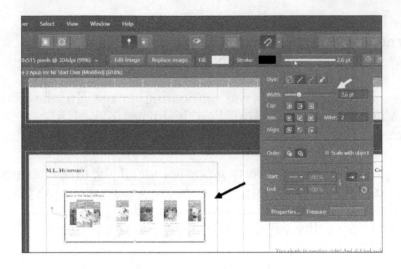

After walking through this here, I have less problem with using pinned images, but I know that I did run into issues properly centering my pinned images when I tried to work with them before. It could've been because of indented paragraphs of text (which can be an issue in Word), but whatever it was I just moved on to picture frames instead of try to get it working consistently.

But pinned images definitely do have the advantage of staying with your text no matter what, so if that's really important for you and your process, absolutely use pinned images instead of picture frames to place your images.

Okay. Next let's talk about image adjustments.

IMAGE ADJUSTMENTS

To wrap this up I want to talk about one final topic and that's making adjustments to your images. This may have something to do with my document and image settings, but I found with the first book that I published using Affinity that my images didn't work well. My paler images were too pale and my darker images were too dark.

Keep in mind that when you set Affinity to grayscale that means the program is converting that image for you behind the scenes. And it seems to me that the way it converts images to grayscale by default may be different from how Word does it, because I never felt the need to make these sorts of adjustments when dealing with images in Word.

I say all of that to basically tell you that you'll need to decide for yourself if your images need adjusting or not. It's quite possible they don't because of your settings or the images you're using. Or you may just be much fancier than me and manually adjust every image to grayscale yourself to make it perfect, which I know some people do.

What I've ended up doing with my Affinity files is take my paler images and darken them and take my darker images and make them lighter. Which means in print some of the images we're about to look at may not look all that great because I want you to see the difference and the adjustments I make.

The top image here is from the fiction layouts Affinity guide without adjustment. The bottom one is that same image with a brightness adjustment applied:

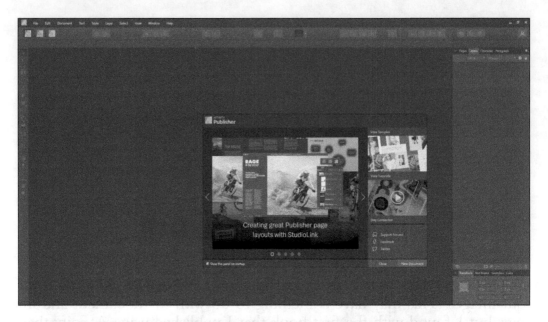

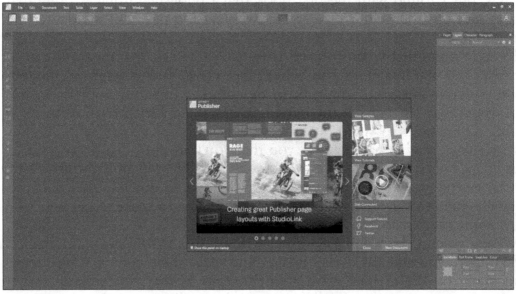

For the ebook version I've done a screenshot of the two to hopefully show the difference.

See how the top image is darker and perhaps a little harder to read or distinguish different components?

Here is an adjustment for an image that's mostly pale lines with the top being the original and the bottom being the adjusted image:

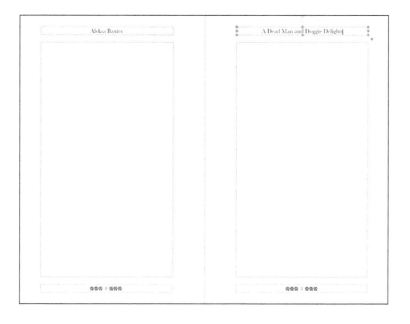

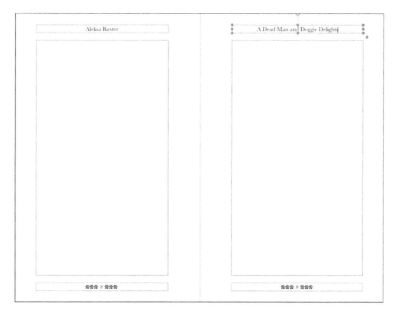

Whether your images will need this sort of adjustment or not is your call. All I can do is tell you to print your document or order a proof copy of your book to see what the images actually look like in print on the page to decide.

If you do decide an adjustments is needed, I use the Brightness and Contrast adjustments option that can be found at the bottom of the studios section:

You can also get there through Layer->New Adjustment in the top menu.

For each of the above I only changed the Brightness level. For the dark images, I used a positive value of about 35% and for the light images I used a negative value of about -25%.

But again, you'll need to find what works for you and your images. For example, I just tried a negative 50% adjustment on that second image and it certainly made those lines much darker, but I'd have to print it to see how the text renders when I do that.

Once you add an adjustment to an image it will show below that image in your Layers studio as a white box with the name of the type of adjustment listed:

You can toggle that adjustment on and off using the checkbox for that adjustment layer.

You can also delete that layer if you want to permanently remove the adjustment. (I sometimes find it easier to remove an adjustment and re-add it rather than try to adjust from where it already is.)

In order to delete just the adjustment layer and not the image as well, be sure to click on the white square for that layer. If you click elsewhere it tends to have a habit of selecting the image layer as well.

Okay, so that's my very basic image adjustment guidance. A true graphic design pro could give you far more guidance on this than I have, but that at least should help you get started with image adjustments.

EXPORT AS PDF

One more topic before we wrap up. We touched on this in prior books, but I want to cover it again, because there's something you need to adjust for if you have a lot of images in your document.

IngramSpark says that they want a PDF/X-1a:2003 file and for fiction layouts that were just using one simple little image that was fine to use in the Affinity export to PDF step. But I found that it didn't work for my books because the images, even if my document was set to be grayscale, exported as color images. Which meant I was leaving the conversion from color to grayscale up to IngramSpark or Amazon.

Not something I was sure I wanted to do. I did with my original Excel books and that worked fine, but why go through the effort of choosing Grayscale in Affinity only to not use it, right?

So what I did was start with that setting in the dropdown and then click on the More option in the dialogue box:

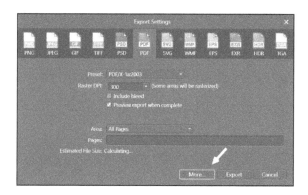

That opened an additional dialogue box:

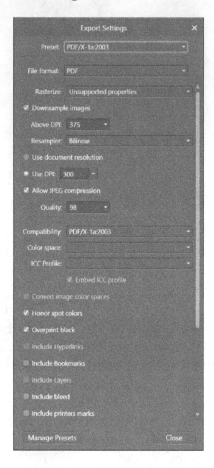

The box I need to have checked is "Convert Image Color Spaces." As you can see here, it's grayed out. I also don't want it to compress JPG images even though I use TIFF images. And you don't want to embed the ICC profile either since that can generate an error message on IngramSpark.

So this is what I end up with:

The first step to get this to all work is to change that Compatibility dropdown to PDF 1.7 which allows for conversion of the image color spaces and makes those checkboxes become available for edit.

I won't promise you that these are the best settings, because I can't. All I can tell you is that if you're reading this in print that they're the settings I used for the book that's in your hands.

Also, note that because I don't want to think about this every single time I export a print book with images in it, that I made it into a preset that's available in my dropdown menu. I did that with the Manage Presets option at the bottom of that larger settings menu.

CONCLUSION

Alright. I think that pretty much covers what I do in Affinity Publisher that's either a more-advanced fiction skill or that's specific to non-fiction. And across this four-book series we've definitely at least touched upon all of the tools and ways in which I use the program.

But as much as I do with Affinity Publisher, I do not have all of the answers. The key when you get stuck is to go find the people who do, which is why I love their forums and product help, because I think they're both very nice to people and provide a lot of solid information.

First, as I mentioned in the first book of this series, the folks at Affinity have excellent instructional videos available on their website: https://affinity.serif.com/en-us/learn/

I watched them all when I was starting out because I didn't know what I didn't know.

The folks at Affinity also have huge, massive, beautiful books they publish on each program that are available through their website and on Amazon and probably every other major retailer.

I am cheap and very bad at following something like that, so I've never bought them, but if their books are the same quality as their product and their videos, then I'd say those are probably worth considering as a resource on your shelf, but I suspect the focus is going to be far different from the focus in these books which was specifically on self-publishing.

I'd expect they're also far more geared towards design professionals who already have that solid graphic design background, but I could be wrong. So maybe check those out.

Also, I use their Affinity Publisher help wiki on a regular basis: https://affinity.help/publisher/en-US.lproj/index.html

Probably not as often as I should. Many of the discoveries I had while writing this book were from there. I'd start to say something here and then think, "Is that really true?" and go find the answer.

Usually their help wiki comes up when I do an internet search for "Affinity Publisher X" where X is what I'm trying to figure out. But you can also navigate through it using the menu options on the side.

And then, last but certainly not least, there are the user forums: https://forum.affinity.serif.com/

That trick I shared here about putting text in a text frame and hiding it behind the book cover to feed your table of contents came from a post there that I happened to see when I was looking for something else.

The forums are another one I've never gone to directly, but have instead found through an internet search. Just keep in mind that from what I can tell this is a product that they've been constantly improving since its original release, so sometimes I'll find an answer from 2018 where someone says you can't do something but it turns out you can now.

So if you see a "that's not an option" answer and it's from more than about six months ago, keep digging to be sure.

And you can always message me, of course. mlhumphreywriter@gmail.com. I'm pretty good at finding answers to things I don't know and then testing them out and gaining an understanding of them.

So even if I don't know the answer when you email me, I'm very likely to go dig it up for you. Just don't abuse that privilege. (I had someone on the Excel side who seemed to think I provide free consulting services for their company who I finally had to cut off.)

Finally, if you want to see the topics that were covered in this book "live", there is a video course version of this book available at https://ml-humphrey.teachable.com/courses. Use code MLH50 to get fifty percent off.

Anyway. I really do like the Affinity suite of products. And I think they really have helped me take things to the next level. I hope the same is true for you.

Good luck with it. And reach out if you get stuck.

APPENDIX A: QUICK TAKES

AUTHOR NAME

FIELD EDIT

Fields studio. Click on field next to Author. Type author name. Enter.

INSERT

Artistic Text Tool. Click on location in document where field should be inserted. Go to Fields studio. Double-click on Author.

BOOK TITLE

FIELD EDIT

Fields studio. Click on field next to Title. Type book title. Enter.

INSERT

Artistic Text Tool. Click on location in document where field should be inserted. Go to Fields studio. Double-click on Title.

CHAPTER TITLE

INSERT AS HEADER

Click on location in document. Go to top menu. Text. Insert Fields. Section Name. Where the chapter title was assigned as the section name.

COLUMNS

BALANCE TEXT

Click on the text frame. Go to the Columns section of the Text Frame studio and click the "Balance Text Columns" box.

CHANGE NUMBER

Click on text frame. Go to dynamic menu up top and change value for Columns.

DIVIDING LINE

Click on the text frame. Open the Text Frame studio and go to the Column Rules section and change the Stroke settings. Top and Bottom values will determine whether the text fills the entire space. Start and End dropdowns can be used to put a shape at the end of the divider line, like an arrow.

FORMAT

Click on the text frame. Open the Text Frame studio and go to the Columns section.

GAP BETWEEN

Click on text frame. Go to dynamic menu up top and change the number in the field to the right of the number of columns setting. Or open the Text Frame studio and go to the Columns section and adjust the value for the gutter there.

EXPORT

PDF

To export a PDF of your document, go to File, Export, and choose the PDF option. For review purposes, All Spreads is better because it will keep facing pages together in the PDF. For KDP and IngramSpark upload, use All Pages.

IMAGE

ADJUSTMENTS

To adjust an image, go to Layer->New Adjustment and choose the type of image adjustment you need. You can also use the Adjustments option at the bottom of the Layers studio to see the list of available adjustments.

CENTER

Left-click and drag the image until you see the green center line. For a standard book, be sure to drag from the outer edge of the page because there will be two center lines, one for the entire page and one for the text frame. For a pinned image, use the Pinning studio.

DPI

The image DPI will increase as your image size decreases.

FLOAT

To float an image, open the Pinning studio and click on the Float tab.

IMPORT PREFERENCES WITH PICTURE FRAME

When importing an image into a picture frame, you can set how the image imports using the Preferences option in the dynamic menu after you click on the picture frame.

INLINE

To make an image an inline image, open the Pinning studio and click on the Inline tab.

INSERT

Place Image Tool. Select image to insert. Open. Image may automatically insert. If not, click and drag in workspace until desired size.

INSERT IN PICTURE FRAME

Click on picture frame layer. Place Image Tool. Select image to insert. Open. Your import preferences will determine if the image comes in at the document DPI or at a size that best fits the picture frame.

MOVE

Move Tool. Click on image layer or directly on image if not in a picture frame. Click on image, hold left-click and drag to desired location. Use snapping to align along edges or center.

MOVE PIN

For a pinned image, you can left-click and drag on the pin to move what text the image is pinned to.

PIN TO TEXT

If you click into your text before inserting an image, the image will be pinned to your text when it inserts. If an image is not pinned to text, you can use the Pinning studio or the pin option in the dynamic menu up top to pin the image to your text after the fact.

QUALITY

For print files, use a DPI of at least 300 for grayscale images and 600 for black and white line drawings. Go to File->Document Setup to specify your document DPI. Set it slightly above the desired DPI if importing images.

REPLACE

Document top menu option. Resource Manager. Select image. Replace. Select new image. Open. Close resource manager. Or, with Move Tool selected, click on image and use Replace Image option in dynamic menu.

RESIZE

Move Tool. Click on image layer or directly on image if not in a picture frame. Option A: Transform studio. Lock Aspect Ratio. Change height or width value. Option B: Click on blue circle in corner and drag at an angle to resize proportionately. Or click on blue circle along any edge to change height or width only. This will skew most images.

UNPIN

Layers studio. Click on image layer. Open Pinning studio. Click on Unpin.

INDEX

INSERT

Click intro document where you want to place the index. Go to the Index studio. Click on the Insert Index option. Or go to the top menu, Text, Index, Insert Index.

MANUAL EDITS

Once inserted, an index can be manually edited but those edits will be overwritten if the index is ever updated.

TEXT STYLE

The index entries use text styles so text can be edited and then the text style updated to apply that change to all entries.

UPDATE

Either go to the top menu and then Text, Index, and Update Index. Or use the Index studio and choose the Update option at the top. If the index does not update, delete the existing text of the index, and insert a new index instead.

INDEX MARKERS AND TOPICS

CROSS-REFERENCE

Both topics need to already exist. Right-click on the topic you want to cross-reference from and choose Add Cross Reference. In the Add Cross-Reference dialogue box select the topic you want to reference to in the dropdown menu.

INSERT

Select the text you want to use as your index text or click into the text where you want the marker. Either go to the Index studio and click on the Insert Marker option at the top or go to the top menu, Text, Index, Insert Index Mark.

MOVE ENTRY LEVEL

Go to the Index studio and left-click on the topic name you want to move. Drag it to the topic you want to place it under. Or, right-click on the topic name choose to Edit Topic, and change the Parent Topic information to either add or remove a parent level.

NAME (ASSIGN)

In the Insert Index Mark dialogue box, type the name into the Topic Name field.

NAME (EDIT)

Click once on the name. Click again to select the text. Type in your new name. Or right-click, Edit Topic, and change the value in the Topic Name field.

PARENT TOPIC (ASSIGN)

The parent topic you want to use needs to be in the index already. When you open the Insert Index Mark dialogue box or the Edit Index Mark dialogue box, choose the parent topic you want from the Parent Topic dropdown menu.

PARENT TOPIC (REMOVE PAGE NUMBERING)

Remove any underlying citations from the Parent Topic in the Index studio. Either move them to the subtopic or delete them using the trash can icon.

MASTER PAGE

ADD NEW

Pages studio. Master Pages section. Right-click on existing master page. Option A: Choose Insert Master. Click OK to create a new master page that has the basic properties of the existing master page. Option B: Choose Duplicate to create an exact duplicate of the existing master page.

MOVE

Pages studio. Master Pages section. Click on master page and drag. Blue line along edge will show where master page will move to. Release left-click when where wanted.

RENAME

Pages studio. Master pages section. Click on master page thumbnail. Click on name of master page. Type in new name. Enter.

MERGE DOCUMENTS

ADD DOCUMENT

Go to the page of the existing document in the Pages studio where you want to add the document, right-click, and choose Add Pages from the dropdown. Navigate to and select the document to import. In the Add Pages dialogue box choose All Pages, After, Pages, and verify that it shows the page number for that page. OK.

PRE-IMPORT SET-UP

If your documents are set to have a right-hand page start, be sure that the document you're importing into has only one page on the left-hand side at the end in order to maintain pages on the correct side of the page.

NEW DOCUMENT PRESET

RENAME

Right-click on thumbnail for preset. Rename Preset. Type new name. OK.

PAGE NUMBER

CHANGE NUMBERING STYLE

Pages studio. Pages section. Right-click on page and choose Edit Section. Click on section name that contains the pages where you want to change the numbering style. Choose the new style from the Number Style dropdown menu. Close.

INSERT

Master page. Artistic Text Tool. Click where you want page number placed. Text top menu choice. Insert. Fields. Page Number.

RESTART AT 1

Pages studio. Pages section. Click on page where you want to restart at 1. Right-click. Start New Section. (Or Edit Section if one has already been started.) Click button for Restart Page Numbering At. Enter 1. Confirm numbering style is correct. If not, choose the correct one from the dropdown menu.

PAGES

ADD PAGES

Pages studio. Pages section. Right-click on an existing page or page spread. Add Pages. Choose the number of pages, whether to insert before or after, the page number (based on left-hand panel numbering where the pages should be inserted), and select the master page to use for the inserted pages. OK.

APPLY MASTER PAGE

Pages studio. Pages section. Right-click on the pages where you want to apply the master page. (Be sure that both pages are selected in a two-page spread.) Apply Master. Choose desired master page from dropdown menu. OK.

DELETE PAGES

Pages studio. Pages section. Click on page or page spread that you want to delete. Right-click. Delete X Pages. If there is more than one page spread that you want to delete, click on page spread at one end of the page range, hold down the shift key and click on the page spread at the other end of the page range. Right-click. Delete X Pages.

PICTURE FRAME

BORDER

Click on the Picture Frame. Go to the dynamic menu up top and change the line width next to the Stroke option.

INSERT

Picture Frame Rectangle Tool. Click and drag to create frame on canvas.

JUMP

To have text jump an inserted picture frame, click on the Picture Frame and then use the Show Text Wrap Settings in the top menu and choose Jump for the Wrap Style.

RESIZE TO IMAGE

Click on Picture Frame and in dynamic menu choose the Size Frame to Content option.

WRAP TEXT AROUND

To have text wrap around an inserted picture frame, click on the Picture Frame and then use the Show Text Wrap Settings in the top menu and choose Square or Tight for the Wrap Style.

RECOVER FILE

RECOVER FILE

If Affinity ever crashes and closes while you were working on a file, reopen the program and try to reopen the file. Affinity should tell you that there is a recovery version of the file available. Choose to open the recovery version and then check for the last edits you made to determine if any of your work was lost and needs to be redone.

SECTION

ASSIGN NAME

Pages studio. Pages section. Right-click and Edit Section. In Section Manager, click on the section that you want to rename. Type name into Section Name field. Close.

CHANGE START PAGE

Pages studio. Pages section. Right-click and Edit Section. In Section Manager, change the "Start On Page".

CONTINUE PAGE NUMBERING

Pages studio. Pages section. Right-click and Edit Section. For the section that needs to continue page numbering, check the box to continue page numbering.

CREATE

Pages studio. Pages section. Right-click on the page that you want to have start the new section, Start New Section. In Section Manager, assign name if desired and verify page numbering format and whether it should restart or continue.

EDIT

Pages studio. Pages section. Right-click and Edit Section.

DELETE

Pages studio. Pages section. Right-click and Edit Section. In Section Manager, click on the section you want to delete and use the small trash can icon to delete it.

INSERT NAME

Click on location in header where field should be inserted. Go to Text top menu option. Insert. Fields. Section Name.

RESTART PAGE NUMBERING

Pages studio. Pages section. Right-click and Edit Section. For the section that needs to restart page numbering, check the box to "restart page numbering at", verify the page number, generally 1, and the number style.

SNAPPING

ENABLE

Go to the horseshoe shaped magnet image in the top center. Click on the dropdown arrow. Check the box next to Enable Snapping.

STUDIO

MOVE OR ANCHOR

Left-click on studio tab and drag to desired location. To anchor, either drag until you see a blue box appear and then release or drag to where other studios are already anchored and add to those tabs.

STUDIO PRESET

ADD NEW

Arrange studios as desired. View top menu option. Studio Presets. Add Preset. Type name. OK.

APPLY

View top menu option. Studio Presets. Select desired preset. Or Ctrl + Shift + [Number].

DELETE

View top menu option. Studio Presets. Manage Studio Presets. Select preset name. Delete. Close.

RENAME

View top menu option. Studio Presets. Manage Studio Presets. Select preset name. Rename. Type in new name. OK. Close.

SAVE CHANGES

Make desired changes to studio preset arrangement. View top menu option. Studio Presets. Add Preset. Type in exact same name as before. OK. Agree to overwrite old preset.

TABLE OF CONTENTS

ENTRIES (INDENT)

Click onto a sample of the text you want to indent in the Table of Contents. Go to the Paragraph studio and set a left indent to the value you want. Update the text style when done.

ENTRIES (SELECT)

Assign one or more unique text styles to each text entry in the document that you want included in the table of contents. Go to the Table of Contents studio and under Style Name, check the check box for each text style you want to include.

ENTRIES (UPDATE)

You can manually update any text in the table of contents, but it is better to update the text in the document and then refresh your table of contents.

ENTRIES (WHEN NO TEXT AVAILABLE FOR SELECTION)

If you ever have a situation where you need a table of contents entry but there is no visible text to use for it, you can create a text frame, place that text you need into the frame, and then hide the frame on the page you need the table of contents entry to start on.

FOR SECTION

To insert a table of contents that covers only a section of a book, insert the table of contents like normal but be sure to check the box for "Stop at Next TOC" and to use different text styles than the ones used in the overarching table of contents.

INSERT

Click into the document where you want your table of contents inserted. Option one, go to the Table of Contents studio, click on the Insert option on the left at the top. Option two, top menu, Text, Table of Contents, Insert Table of Contents.

OVERARCHING

For a table of contents that covers the entire document when other tables of contents exist in the document, be sure to use specific text styles for just that table of contents and to NOT check the "Stop at Next TOC" option.

PAGE NUMBERS

To include page numbers, right-click on the preferences dropdown for that text style and check the box for "Include Page Number." To remove page numbers, uncheck it.

SEPARATORS BETWEEN TEXT AND PAGE NUMBER

Go to the Separator section of the Table of Contents studio. Use the dropdown menu to select your desired separator or type into the field. For a dotted line, right-click on the text style and choose to edit it. Go to the Tab Stops section and choose the Tab Stop Leader Character option that has a period in the parens.

UPDATE

Go to the Table of Contents studio and click on the Update option at the top. If you have multiple tables of contents in your document, be sure the TOC dropdown shows the table of contents you want to update or choose to update all. Or go to Text, Table of Contents, Update Table of Contents or click on Fix in the Preflight studio.

TEXT

ADD SPACE BETWEEN LINES

Artistic Text Tool. Select paragraph of text. Paragraph studio. Spacing section. Leading dropdown. Choose desired option. Or for multiple lines of the same style, click on Space Between Same Styles and set a value.

ADD SPECIAL SYMBOLS OR CHARACTERS

Artistic Text Tool. Click into workspace where desired. Go to View top menu. Studio. Glyph Browser. Or if docked, open glyph browser. Find desired symbol or character. Double-click on symbol or character to insert.

ALIGNMENT

Artistic Text Tool. Click on the paragraph or paragraphs. Menu choices above workspace. Four images with lines. Align Left, Align Center, Align Right, or dropdown menu for Justify Left, Justify Center, Justify Right, Justify All, Align Towards Spine, Align Away From Spine. Or, to the right of that, dropdown menu for Top Align, Center Vertically, Bottom Align, Justify Vertically. The horizontal alignment options are also available at the top of the Paragraph studio.

ALL CAPS OR SMALL CAPS

Artistic Text Tool. Select the text to be formatted. Go to Character studio. Typography section. Click on the two capital Ts (TT) to apply all caps. Click on the capital T with a smaller capital T (TT) to apply small caps. Check your text entries for issues with using a capital letter or lower case letter when working with small caps because the two do look different in small caps.

APPLY HYPHENATION

Artistic Text Tool. Select text. Paragraph studio. Hyphenation section. Click on box next to Use Auto-Hyphenation. Change values as needed.

APPLY TRACKING

Artistic Text Tool. Select text. Character studio. Positioning and Transform section. Second option in the left-hand column, Tracking. Click arrow for dropdown menu. Choose desired change.

BOLD

Artistic Text Tool. Select text. Ctrl + B. Or click on B in top menu. Or go to Character studio and choose the Strong option from the Style dropdown menu at the top. Only works if there is a bold version of the font available.

FONT

Artistic Text Tool. Select text. Top menu, left-hand side. Font dropdown. Choose font. Or select text and go to Character studio font dropdown at top.

INDENT PARAGRAPH

Artistic Text Tool. Select paragraph. Paragraph studio. Spacing section. Second option on left-hand side. (First Line Indent). Add value.

ITALICS

Artistic Text Tool. Select text. Ctrl + I. Or click on I in top menu. Or go to Character studio and choose the Emphasis option from the Style dropdown menu at the top. Only works if there is an italic version of the font available.

JUMP IMAGE

Move Tool. Select image. Click on Show Text Wrap Settings option in top menu. In Text Wrap dialogue box choose Jump as desired Wrap Style.

KEEP TOGETHER

Artistic Text Tool. Select second paragraph or line that you want to keep together. Go to the Paragraph studio. Flow Options section. Check box for Keep With Previous Paragraph.

LINE SPACING (LEADING)

Artistic Text Tool. Select paragraph. Paragraph studio. Spacing section. Change value in Leading dropdown. Default is usually a good place to start.

MOVE TO NEXT PAGE

Click right after the text that's before the text you want to move to the next page. Go to Text->Insert->Break->Frame Break to move the text to the next frame.

ORPHANS REMOVE AUTOMATICALLY

Artistic Text Tool. Select text. Paragraph studio. Flow Options. Check box for Prevent Orphaned First Lines.

SIZE

Artistic Text Tool. Select text. Top menu, left-hand side. Font size dropdown. Choose size or type in size. Or select text and go to Character studio font size dropdown at top.

SMALL CAPS

See *All Caps or Small Caps.*

UNDERLINE

Artistic Text Tool. Select text. Ctrl + U. Or click on the underlined U in top menu. Or go to Character studio and choose one of the underlined U options from the Decorations section.

WEIGHT

Artistic Text Tool. Select text. Top menu, left-hand side. Font weight dropdown. Choose from available weights for that font. Or select text and go to Character studio font weight dropdown at top.

WIDOWS REMOVE AUTOMATICALLY

Artistic Text Tool. Select text. Paragraph studio. Flow Options. Check box for Prevent Widowed Last Lines.

WRAP AROUND IMAGE

Move Tool. Select image. Click on Show Text Wrap Settings option in top menu. In Text Wrap dialogue box choose Wrap Style.

TEXT FLOW

AUTO FLOW

Pages studio. Pages section. Double-click on last page spread in section. Go to right-hand edge of last text frame in workspace. Click on red circle to see red arrow. Hold down shift key and click on red arrow. Affinity will flow the text to as many page spreads as needed using the same master page spread format.

FROM ONE TEXT FRAME TO ANOTHER ADD

Click on blue arrow along the edge of the first text frame. Click on second text frame.

FROM ONE TEXT FRAME TO ANOTHER REMOVE

Click on the blue arrow along the edge of the first text frame. Click back onto the first text frame.

TEXT FRAME

ALIGN OR POSITION

Frame Text Tool or Move Tool. Left-click on text frame and hold as you drag. Look for red and green alignment lines to center or align to other elements in workspace. (Turn on Snapping if there are no red or green lines.)

INSERT

Frame Text Tool on left-hand side. Click and drag in workspace.

TEXT STYLE

APPLY

Artistic Text Tool. Select text. Use dropdown menu at top to apply style. Or go to Text Styles studio and click on desired style. Or use shortcut if one is associated with the style.

BASED ON OTHER STYLE

To base a text style off of another style, first apply the existing text style. Next, make any edits to create the new style. And then save as new style.

IMPORTED

If you use the import text style option or are merging two files and it appears, you can choose which text styles to import using the checkbox on the far left. If this is for an import with overlapping text style names click on the Rename To option to bring in the text style but with a new name, click on OK to bring it in with the same name, or choose which of the two styles to keep if there is a conflict identified.

KEYBOARD SHORTCUT

For a new style, add keyboard shortcut in the Style section of the Create Paragraph Style dialogue box where it says Keyboard Shortcut. (Don't type the description, just use the shortcut when you're clicked into the box.) For an existing style, go to the Text Styles studio, right-click on the style name, Edit [Style Name], and then in the Style section of the Edit Text Style dialogue box, add the keyboard shortcut.

NEW

Artistic Text Tool. Select text. Format text. Text style dropdown in top menu. New Style. Give style a name and keyboard shortcut if desired. OK.

UPDATE OR CHANGE

Artistic Text Tool. Select text with style to be updated. Make edits. Click on paragraph symbol with a swish that's to the right of the text style dropdown menu in the top menu area. Or, go to Text Styles studio, right-click on text style name, Edit [Style Name], make edits in Edit Text Style dialogue box, OK.

INDEX

ABOUT THE AUTHOR

M.L. Humphrey is a self-published author with both fiction and non-fiction titles published under a variety of pen names. When she gets stuck on her next fiction project she foolishly decides to write books that only ten people are going to buy, although she does usually learn something interesting in the process so it's worth it in the end.

You can reach her at:

mlhumphreywriter@gmail.com

or at

www.mlhumphrey.com

www.ingramcontent.com/pod-product-compliance
Lightning Source LLC
Chambersburg PA
CBHW060150060326
40690CB00018B/4054